W. H. Mansfield and Co.

The Mansfield Cook Book

A Careful Compilation of Treid and True Recipes

W. H. Mansfield and Co.

The Mansfield Cook Book
A Careful Compilation of Treid and True Recipes

ISBN/EAN: 9783744788731

Printed in Europe, USA, Canada, Australia, Japan

Cover: Foto ©Lupo / pixelio.de

More available books at **www.hansebooks.com**

नरक

Austin, Nichols & Co's

FARINACEOUS GOODS ARE UNEXCELLED.

Alexander Cairns' Jams and Jellies are put up in Paisley, Scotland, from fruit grown in the Clydesdale orchards; and we assure you that Mr. Cairns enjoys the highest reputation of any manufacturer in his line in Great Britain, which an experience of forty years has given him.

```
        etables
        ies
do      Olive Oil
do      French Olives
```

The above for sale by

W. H. MANSFIELD & CO,

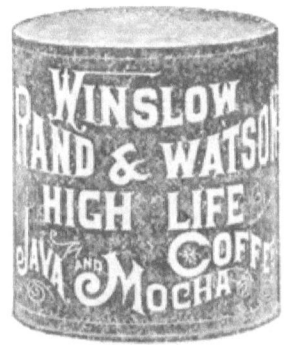

COFFEES

One and Two lb. Cans

WINSLOW, RAND & WATSON,

Importers and Jobbers of

─✱─ Teas, ✱ Coffees, ─✱─

and Roasters of Coffee,

197 AND 199 STATE ST., BOSTON.

──(:OUR SPECIALTIES ARE:)──

PURITY JAVA,

    PURITY JAVA and MOCHA,

        HIGH LIFE JAVA and MOCHA

We sincerely believe that the quality of these Coffees is far superior to any ever offered for sale in Windham County. Their absolute purity and delicacy of flavor, have won for them a national reputation; their drinking qualities are extra fine; they draw heavy and still retain their high flavor in the cup, which is peculiar to these brands alone. High Life Mocha and Java is sold only in one and two pound air tight cans, and every label bears our signature.

── FOR SALE BY ──

W. H. Mansfield & Co.,

And other leading grocers in Connecticut.

Important to the Public!

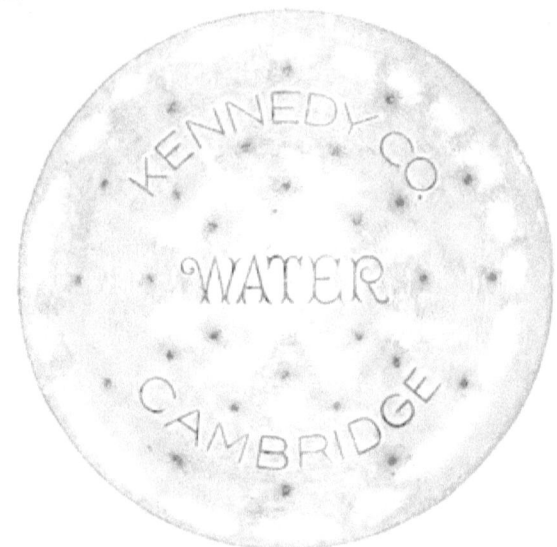

KENNEDY'S THIN WATERS

Are the original and only genuine Thin Water Wafer on the market. Packed attractively in one and two pound boxes. Always ask for Kennedy's.

———— MANUFACTURERS OF ————

ALL KINDS OF FANCY BISCUITS!

Zephyrs, Champions, Graham Wafers, Oatmeal Wafers, Butter Wafers, Jockey Clubs, Cream Wafers, Saltines, Cambridge Salts, Alberts, Oswegos, and a line of Sweet Biscuits too large to enumerate.

Orange, Vanilla, Strawberry, Lemon, and Ginger WAFERS packed in handsome one pound cans.

The Best Goods in the World.

F. A. KENNEDY CO.,

Cambridgeport, Chicago, New York, Washington, Philadelphia, St. Paul, Minneapolis.

All the above named Biscuits sold by

W. H. MANSFIELD & CO., Putnam

THE MANSFIELD COOK BOOK.

A Careful Compilation of Tried and True Recipes.

Copyright, 1890, by W. H. Mansfield & Co.

PUBLISHED BY

W. H. MANSFIELD & CO.,

THE GROCERS.

Cor. Main and Pomfret Sts., Putnam, Conn

"We may live without poetry, music and art;
We may live without conscience, and live without heart;
We may live without friends; we may live without books;
But civilized man cannot live without cooks."

PUTNAM, CONN.:
THE PATRIOT PRESS.
1890.

VICTOR FLOUR

Is the Best !

And will continue to be the Best.

Victor will be the best under all circumstances.

Some other brands of flour may sometimes make as good bread, but for reliability and uniformity the Victor will be the victor, as it has been the victor for the past 14 years.

Always trouble in the family without good bread in the house.

Its enormous sales are due to the fact that the best cooks always use the Victor.

Don't spend your time, money, patience and material in trying to match the Victor with other so called "best brands."

W. H. MANSFIELD & CO.,

Putnam, Conn.,

Mill Agents for Windham County.

SOUPS.

All meats and bones for soup should be boiled a long time, and then set aside until the next day, in order that the fat may be removed. Then add the vegetables, rice or herbs from an hour to an hour and a half. A slight addition of Tournade's Kitchen Bouquet adds greatly to the flavor and color, for many of the following recipes.

TO PREPARE SOUP STOCK.

Five pounds from a leg of beef, three pounds from a shoulder of lamb, three pounds from a leg of veal. Boil gently five hours, putting in one onion and one stalk of celery. Boil another hour and then strain, adding salt and pepper. This is ready for clear soup or for the foundation of other soups.

CREAM OF BARLEY SOUP.

One teacup of pearl barley well washed, three pints of chicken or veal clear stock, one onion. Cook slowly together for four or five hours; add one and a half pints of boiling milk, two tablespoonfuls of butter, and three well beaten eggs, salt and pepper to taste. Let it stay on the stove for a few minutes after the milk, eggs and butter are added, but do not let it boil.

TOMATO SOUP.

One quart of soup stock, one can of Old Reliable tomatoes, or one quart stewed tomatoes, four dessert spoons of sugar, salt to taste, a little grated nutmeg, four large tablespoonfuls of flour, three large tablespoonfuls of butter, rubbed smooth and stirred in to thicken. Strain on to cubes of fried bread or browned bread, a little pepper.

BOUILLON

Six pounds beef and bone, soup bones, for ten persons; cut up the meat and break the bones, add two quarts of cold water and let it simmer slowly until all the strength is exhausted from the meat; it will take about four hours. Straie through a fine sieve, removing every particle of fat, and if there is more than ten cupfuls reduce it by boiling to that quantity; season with salt and pepper only. It is served in bouillon cups at luncheon and evening companies.

Use Victor Flour and be Happy

SOUP A L'OIGNON.

Slice fine four large white onions, put into a stewpan with four ounces of butter, stir and fry slowly until softened and slightly browned; besprinkle with two ounces of sifted flour, dilute with two quarts of beef broth and a quart of water, add salt and pepper and boil ten minutes. Meanwhile cut in thin slices, and dry in the oven about four ounces of bread; have a well-buttered soup tureen bestrewn with grated Parmesan cheese, put in a layer of bread, sprinkle grated cheese over, add two more layers of each, finishing with the cheese; pour the boiling soup over, cover for a few minutes to give time for the cheese to melt and the bread to soak, and serve. The onions may also be strained without imparing the flavor and richness of the soup, and before serving add a teaspoonful of Tournade's Kitchen Bouquet.

TOMATO SOUP.

Three pints of tomatoes, stewed and strained, a little sugar, one onion, two quarts of beef stock, salt and pepper.

CROUTSONS.

Slice yeast bread and spread with butter on both sides. Cut in small squares and brown in the oven very quickly. To be served with soup.

MOCK BISQUE SOUP.

A can of Old Reliable tomatoes, three pints of milk, one large tablespoon of flour, butter the size of an egg, pepper and salt to taste, a scant teaspoon of soda. Put the tomato on to stew, and the milk in a double boiler to boil, reserving half a cupful to mix with flour. Mix the flour smoothly with the cold milk, stir into the boiling milk, and cool ten minutes. To the tomato add the soda; stir well and strain. Add butter, salt and pepper to the milk, and then to the tomatoes.

CREAM OF CELERY SOUP.

One quart of milk, two tablespoonfuls of flour, two of butter, two heads of celery, and a little mace. Boil celery in a pint of water for an hour; boil mace and milk together. Mix flour with two tablespoonfuls of cold milk and add to boiling milk. Cook ten minutes. Mash celery in the water

Old Reliable Tomatoes are the BEST

in which it has been cooked and stir into boiling milk. Add butter, and season with salt and pepper. Strain and serve immediately. It is much improved by adding a half cup of whipped cream.

FISH CHOWDER NO. 1.

Take three pounds of fish, either cod or haddock, corned fish I prefer, five potatoes and two onions. Put them on and boil one hour in a pint and a half of water. Cut your fish in small pieces, then put together and cook until done. Add three crackers and cook fifteen minutes, lastly one quart of milk heated to boiling point, a half cup of powdered crackers in milk, one-fourth pound of pork or butter, pepper to taste.

FISH CHOWDER NO. 2.

For a fish of four pounds, take ten potatoes, one pint of milk, three pints of water and about four slices of pork. Cut the pork in small pieces and try out all the fat, using only the fat in the chowder, or use butter if you wish. Slice the potatoes and put on in the water, when they begin to grow soft, put in the fish (cut up in pieces) and cook for twenty minutes. Just before taking from the stove add the milk, and salt and pepper to taste.

CLAM STEW

Put two quarts of milk on to scald and have heating at the same time one quart of clams. Add about one half pound of butter and season to taste with salt and pepper. Do not cook any after putting in the clams.

TURKEY SOUP.

Take the remnants of a turkey (say left from dinner), add to them two or three quarts of water, boil two hours.

JULIENNE SOUP.

Take two medium sized carrots, a medium sized turnip, a piece of celery, the core of a lettuce, and an onion. Cut them into strips about an inch long. Fry the onions in butter without allowing it to take color, add the carrots, turnips and celery, raw, if tender; if not boil them separately for a few minutes; after frying all for a few minutes, season with a pinch of salt and a teaspoonful of sugar, then moisten with a gill of broth; boil until reduced to a glaze, add two quarts

We Sell Tournade's Kitchen Bouquet and recommend it

of good stock skimmed, and put through sieve, and remove the stew pan to the back of the stove so that it may boil only partially; quarter of an hour after add the lettuce which has been boiled in other water; boil all together.

BISQUE OF LOBSTER.

Two pounds of lobster, one quart of milk, one tablespoon of butter, two tablespoons of flour or corn starch, one teaspoonful of salt, one teaspoonful of white pepper, one quarter of cayenne pepper, one pint of water. Cut the tender pieces of lobster into quarter inch dice. Put the claw meat and any tough part with the bones of the body into a pint of cold water, boil twenty minutes, add water as it boils away. Put the coral on paper, dry in the oven. Boil one quart of milk, thicken it with the flour and butter. Boil ten minutes, strain the water from the bones and add to the milk, with salt and pepper. Rub the dry coral through a strainer and use enough to give the soup a bright pink color, pour over the dice in a tureen.

PEA SOUP.

One pint of split peas, let them stand over night in cold water, strain in the morning, pour cold water over them, and boil until the peas are like jelly; add one slice of pork; cook two hours.

VEGETABLE SOUP.

Boil a beef bone two hours; add salt, strain and put with this, chopped fine, five cents worth of soup vegetables; boil all together three quarters of an hour.

TURTLE BEAN SOUP.

One pint black beans soaked in water over night, add one gallon water, half pound salt pork, half pound beef one onion and a grated carrot; strain after boiling three or four hours. Put a little wine, one lemon and a hard boiled egg, sliced in a tureen. Pour the soup over them.

POTATO SOUP.

A quart of milk, six large potatoes, one stalk of celery, an onion, and a tablespoonful of butter. Put milk to boil with onion and celery; pare potatoes and boil thirty minutes,

Old Reliable Corn always pleases

drain and mash fine. Add boiling milk and butter, pepper and salt to taste. Rub through a strainer and serve immediately. A cupful of whipped cream, added when in the tureen is a great improvement. This soup must not be allowed to stand, not even if kept hot. Serve as soon as ready. It is excellent.

NOODLE SOUP.

Four pounds of veal boiled till tender, three eggs well beaten, with enough flour stirred in to make a very stiff dough; roll the dough to thinness of a wafer and dry; roll up the sheet and cut in shavings; stir into soup fifteen minutes before serving.

CHICKEN SOUP.

Two chickens boiled in two quarts of water until the meat will fall from the bones. Take meat from the soup, leave the bones and boil one hour longer; then strain through an old napkin and put on to boil with two tablespoons of pearl barley; boil until soft, then strain and add one-half cup of cream with a small teaspoon of flour. Scald, not boil, and then serve.

CORN SOUP.

One can of Old Reliable corn, chopped fine, one quart of milk, one pint of hot water, one heaping tablespoonful of flour, two tablespoonfuls of butter, one slice of onion, salt and pepper to taste. Cook the corn in the water thirty minutes; let the milk and onion come to a boil; have the flour and butter mixed together and add a few tablespoonfuls of boiling milk; when perfectly smooth stir into the milk and cook eight minutes. Take out the onion and the corn. Let boil up and strain through a coarse sieve or colander and send to table.

BROWN SOUP.

One large beef shank, one carrot, one turnip, two onions, a handful of pepper corns. Boil all together in cold water slowly all day. Skim and strain the next day and put on stove. Add one white and one egg shell, boil five minutes, strain through a fine cloth and let it settle all day. Heat before dinner and add a glass of wine and rings of egg.

Ask Your Grocer for Sample of Kitchen Bouquet.

— USE TOURNADE'S —
Kitchen Bouquet.

Indispensable to Families, Hotels, and Restaurants.

First Class Gold Medal Awarded At the Culinary Exposition, held in New York May, 1882.

Acknowledged the best article of its kind by Proprietors and Chief Cooks of the most prominent Hotels in New York.

SOLD BY ALL FIRST CLASS GROCERS.

Owing to the advance in the art of cooking, this article has rapidly become a household necessity, and is daily growing in popular esteem. It imparts to

Soups, Gravies and Sauces a Delicious Fragrance,

As well as a Rich, Brilliant Color, and being a liquid, dissolves instantly. We guarantee its safe keeping in any climate, and absolute wholesomeness. Approved by the **Liebig Extract of Meat Company.**

TESTIMONIALS.

NEW YORK, September 4th, 1876.

J. L. TOURNADE, ESQ.,

DEAR SIR,—Your KITCHEN BOUQUET is an excellent thing, which I will use, and also take pleasure in recommending.

Very truly yours,
C. B. WAITE,
Proprietor Brevoort House and Windsor Hotel.

It affords me pleasure to inform you that I have used your KITCHEN BOUQUET, and found it of a superior quality. According to my judgment, it will become a necessity in all good cooking.

E. LAPERRUQUE,
Chief Cook at Delmonico's.

Having used your KITCHEN BOUQUET, I desire to say that its qualities have a great superiority over any article ever offered for the same object. I will recommend its use always and on every occasion.

SEB. MICHEL,
Chief, Hotel Brunswick.

We take pleasure in stating that your KITCHEN BOUQUET is a most excellent article, and the superiority of its qualities in flavoring and in giving a good and brilliant color ought to render it of great utility in all good cooking, not only in hotels and restaurants, but also on steamers and in private families, where, in our opinion, it will be of great service. We highly recommend it:

LOUIS RAGOT	Chief,	Delmonico.
HENRY HUGUES	"	Albemarle Hotel.
CHAS. FISCHER	"	St. Nicholas Hotel.
EDOUARD MEHL	"	Gilsey House.
AUG. VALADON	"	St. James Hotel.
FELIX DELIEE	"	Manhattan Club.
J. LUDIN	"	New York Hotel.
C. F. CAGLIERESI	"	Metropolitan Hotel.
GUSTAVE FEROUD	"	Fifth Avenue Hotel.
LEON CHEROT	"	Westminster Hotel.
J. B. PEYROUX	"	Everett House.
GUSTAVE NOUVEL	"	Hoffman House.

Opinion of Leading Grocers.

NEW YORK, February 21st, 1882.

Having sold and used different Flavorings and French Pastilles, for Flavoring and Coloring Soups, etc., we hereby recommend **Tournade's Kitchen Bouquet** as being decidedly superior to all others.

E. C. Hazard & Co., Jas. P. Smith, Bogle & Lyles,
Austin, Nichols & Co., Francis H. Leggett & Co.,
Park & Tilford, Acker, Merrall & Condit.

FISH.

Purchase those which have just been caught; of this you can judge by their being hard under the pressure of the finger. Cod is best in cold weather. Mackerel is best in August, September and October. Halibut in May and June. Oysters are good from September to April. Lobsters are best at the season when oysters are not good. Fish that is to be fried should be cut up and laid in a cloth for an hour in order that the moisture may be absorbed, season with pepper and salt, then roll in fine bread crumbs or corn meal, and fry in one-third butter and two-thirds lard. That which is apt to break in frying may be kept whole by being dipped in a beaten egg before it is rolled in crumbs.

TO BOIL SALT COD.

Let it stand over night in cold water. Put in a kettle, let it set where it will keep warm and at length simmer but not boil.

TO BOIL HALIBUT.

Purchase a thick slice, cut through the body or tail-piece which is considered the richest, wrap it in a flannel cloth and lay in cold water with salt in it. A piece weighing six pounds should cook half an hour after the water boils.

TO BOIL SALMON.

Clean a salmon in salt and water, allow twenty minutes for boiling every pound; wrap in a floured cloth and lay in a kettle while the water is cold, make the water very salt, and skim it well. In this respect it requires more care than any other fish.

TO BOIL FRESH COD.

Rub the fish with salt, wrap it in a cloth, and put it over the fire in cold water enough to cover the fish, adding one tablespoonful of salt; take off the froth and boil half an hour.

Cracker Crumbs Always in Stock.

TO BAKE FISH.

Make a dressing of chopped bread, pepper, salt, butter, and pulverized sage, moisten it with a little water; lay this inside the fish, sew it up, put a skewer through the lip and tail, fasten them together with a piece of twine, lay it in a dish, put two or three thin slices of salt pork upon it, sprinkle salt over it and flour well. Baste with the liquid which cooks out of it. A fish weighing four pounds will cook in an hour.

TO BROIL SALMON.

Cut in slices an inch thick, dry it in a cloth, salt it, lay upon a hot gridiron, the bars having been rubbed with lard or drippings. It cooks very well in a stove oven, laid in a dripping pan.

TO FRY OYSTERS.

Lay them in a cloth a few minutes to dry, then dip each one in beaten eggs, then in sifted cracker crumbs, and fry in just enough fat to brown them. Put pepper and salt on them before you turn them over.

FRICASSEE OF OYSTERS.

Put one quart of oysters on the fire, in their liquor. The moment they begin to boil turn them into a hot dish, through a colander, leaving the oysters in the colander. Put in the saucepan butter the size of an egg, and when it bubbles up, sprinkle in a tablespoonful of sifted flour; let it cook a minute without taking color, stirring it well with a wire egg whisk, then add one cup of oyster liquor. Take it from the fire and mix in the yolks of two eggs, a little salt, a little cayenne pepper, one teaspoonful of lemon juice, and one grated nutmeg; beat it well; then return to the fire to set the eggs without allowing it to boil. Put in the oysters.

SCALLOPED OYSTERS.

Crush or roll several handfuls of oyster crackers, put a layer in the bottom of a buttered pudding dish, wet this with milk slightly warm; next a layer of oysters sprinkled with salt, pepper, and bits of butter, then another layer of cracker crumbs, moistened with milk, and so on until your dish is

Try Those Nice Mackerel

filled. Let the top be of crumbs. Put bits of butter over it and bake an hour; ornament with split crackers.

OYSTER PATTIES.

Line patty-pans with a rich paste, put a piece of bread in each to keep them in shape, bake, and, when cool, turn them out upon a dish. Stew a pint of oysters one or two minutes in their own liquor. Turn on the liquor; put two or three oysters in each puff and cover with hot asparagus dressing. Serve immediately.

CLAMS IN CREAM.

Put butter size of an egg into a spider with a tablespoon of flour. Stir and cook slowly but not to brown. Add one-half cup of clam water. When this comes to a boil add one pint of chopped clams. Just before serving add one cup of cream, being careful that it does not come to a boil after the cream is put in. Pepper to taste.

SALT FISH BALLS No. 1.

One cup of raw salt fish, three cups of boiled potatoes, one tablespoon of melted butter, one tablespoon of sweet milk, one egg, a little pepper. Wash the fish and pick from the bones; put in cold water and let it stand on the back of the stove until fresh enough. Mash or beat the fish and potatoes until light, make in little balls, roll in flour and fry in plenty of hot fat.

FISH BALLS No. 2.

Boil the potatoes, and while still hot peel and mash them. Then to each four cupfuls of potatoes add two cupfuls of fish previously chopped fine, one egg, a piece of butter the size of an egg. Work thoroughly with the hands, adding at the same time milk enough to mold well, and season with salt and pepper to suit the taste. Roll into balls and fry brown on both sides. Serve hot.

SCALLOPED CLAMS.

Put stale bread in oven to dry, roll fine, then put in a dish a layer of crumbs, then a layer of clams, cut in small pieces, season with butter and pepper, so on until the dish is full. Pour the clam water over it and bake one hour. Rolled

Genuine Codfish Constantly on Hand.

crackers may be used in place of bread and also milk with the clam water.

CLAM FRITTERS.

One pint of flour, one-half pint of milk, two eggs, one teaspoon of salt, one large spoon of melted butter, one quart of chopped clams.

BAKED LOBSTER IN THE SHELL.

Take two small lobsters, one-half pint of milk, one small onion chopped fine, butter size of a large egg, three tablespoonfuls flour, cooked all together; remove from the fire and stir in one well beaten egg; add a very little cayenne pepper, and salt if necessary. The green of the lobster must be added to the dressing when cold. Put the chopped lobster into the dish in which it is to be served or into the shells; pour over the dressing slowly until all is thoroughly moistened; then sprinkle cracker crumbs over the top. Bake fifteen minutes. Serve (if in the shells) on a napkin garnished with parsley.

SARDINE SANDWICHES.

One slice of bread, buttered and halved, remove the crust. Split a sardine and remove the bone. Put on one-half a slice, sprinkle a little lemon juice over it and cover with the other half.

TURBOT A LA CREME.

Boil three or four pounds of haddock; take out all the bones and shred the fish fine. Let a quart of milk and a small onion come to a boil; stir in a scant cupful of flour which has been mixed with a cup of cold milk and the yolks of two eggs. Season with one-half teaspoon of white pepper, one teaspoon salt, a small piece of butter. Butter a pan, put in a layer of fish, then one of sauce; finish with the sauce and over it sprinkle cracker crumbs. Bake an hour in a moderate oven.

LOBSTER FARCE.

One cup of cream; put over a double boiler. Put two large spoonfuls of butter into a sauce-pan, when melted add dessert spoon of flour, a little cayenne pepper, mace and salt;

Genuine French Sardines always in Stock

stir into hot cream and let it boil up. This is enough for three pounds of lobster picked to pieces. Fill lobster shells (the back of the lobsters) with the mixture, cover with crumbs, butter and brown. Serve hot.

SALMON.

One can of salmon, three eggs, four tablespoons of melted butter, one-half cup of fine bread crumbs, one-third of a cup of milk; pepper and salt. Pick up the fish, drain off the oil, melt butter, work in the bread crumbs and seasoning, and last of all the eggs. Put in a buttered dish and steam for one hour.

SALMON IN SHELLS.

Two pounds of salmon, boiled tender, one cup of milk, one heaping tablespoonful of butter, two of flour dredged dry on the salmon. Heat milk and butter, mince all together, fill in shells, set in cold water and leave in oven long enough to brown; a quick oven is best; a little cracker dust over each shell and a small piece of butter before putting in oven.

PICKED UP FISH.

One cup of salt fish, shredded or cut across the grain; soak in warm water and cook until it is tender and fresh enough to use. Add a large spoon of butter, and pepper to taste, and then add a cup of hot cream thickened with a little corn starch.

TABLE DELICACIES

Olives, Olive Oil, Dressings, Sauces, Pickles, Preserves, Jellies, Mustards, Relishes, Catsups, French Vinegars, Capers, Sardines, and in fact a full line always on hand at

W. H. Mansfield & Co.'s

SAUCES

FOR MEAT, FISH AND POULTRY.

OYSTER SAUCE.

Two tablespoonfuls of flour, two tablespoonfuls of butter, brown the butter and flour in a dipper; add water to make it thin as gravy, boil; add one pint of oysters, whole pepper and salt. Serve with turkey.

CHICKEN SAUCE.

Put butter the size of an egg into a sauce pan, when it bubbles add a tablespoonful of flour; cook, add a pint of boiling water, when smooth take from the fire, add the beaten yolks of two eggs and a few drops of lemon juice.

TOMATO SAUCE FOR CHOPS AND CROQUETTS.

One can of Old Reliable tomatoes, half of an onion, six or eight cloves. Boil half an hour, then take two tablespoonfuls of butter and two of flour. Put on the fire and stir until brown, then mix with other ingredients and let all boil up once. Strain through a sieve.

BREAD SAUCE FOR GAME.

Two cupfuls of milk, one of dried bread crumbs, a quarter of an onion, two tablespoonfuls of butter, and salt and pepper. Dry the bread in a warm oven, and roll into rather coarse crumbs. Sift, and put the fine crumbs which come through and which make about one-third of a cupful on to boil with the milk and onion. Boil ten or fifteen minutes and add a tablespoon of butter and the seasoning. Skim out the onion. Fry the coarse crumbs a light brown in the remaining butter, which must be very hot before they are put in. Stir over a hot oven two minutes, being watchful not to burn. Cover the breast of the roasted birds with

Use Mansfield's Pure Spices.

these and serve the sauce poured around the birds or in a gravy dish.

DRAWN BUTTER SAUCE.

Three ounces of butter, one ounce of flour, half a pint of water, little salt and pepper. Put two ounces of the butter in a pan; when it bubbles, add flour; stir it well with a wire egg whisk, do not let it color; then add the water. Put it through a sieve and add the other ounce of butter cut in pieces. Add three hard boiled eggs chopped. Serve with meat or fish.

MINT SAUCE.

Mix one tablespoonful of white sugar to one-half a cup of vinegar; add mint chopped fine and half a teaspoonful of salt. Serve with roast lamb or mutton.

CREAM SAUCE NO. 1.

One pint of hot cream, or milk, two even tablespoonfuls of butter, two heaping tablespoonfuls of corn starch, one-half teaspoonful of salt, one-half a saltspoonful of white pepper, one-half a teaspoonful of celery salt, a few grains of cayenne pepper. Scald the cream, melt the butter in a granite sauce pan, when bubbling add the dry corn starch, stir until well mixed, add one third the cream and stir as it boils and thickens; add more cream and boil again; when smooth add the remainder of the cream and seasoning.

Mix with the chicken in making croquettes.

CREAM SAUCE TO BE SERVED WITH CROQUETTES.

One pint of cream or milk, one heaping tablespoon of butter, two heaping tablespoons flour, one-half teaspoon salt one-half saltspoon of pepper. Make same as cream sauce No. 1.

MUSHROOM SAUCE.

One can of mushrooms, two cups of soup stock, two tablespoons of flour, four tablespoons of butter, sa't and pepper. Melt the butter; add the flour and stir until a dark brown; add the stock gradually. When it boils add the liquor from the mushrooms; season and simmer twenty minutes. Skim off the fat that rises; add the mushrooms and simmer five minutes. Serve with beef steak.

Butter, Cheese and Eggs a Specialty

POULTRY.

If care is taken in picking and dressing fowls and birds, there is no need of washing them.

ROAST TURKEY.

First dress it. Season well. Sprinkle pepper and salt on the inside. Stuff it and tie well in shape. Wet the skin in water and sprinkle with pepper, salt and flour. Pour a little boiling water in the pan. Baste it often and cook three or four hours according to size.

ROAST TURKEY, GIBLET SAUCE.

Select a large, tender, dry-picked turkey-hen, singe, draw and truss nicely; cover the breast with a slice of fat salt pork and roast about an hour and a quarter; untie, dish up, pour the drippings over and serve with the following sauce:

Boil until done, in a pint of broth, the heart and gizzard of the turkey, boil the liver in fat for five minutes; drain and slice the whole; slightly thicken the broth with a little flour and butter. Boil ten minutes, skim, add the sliced giblet, season to taste, with the addition of 1-2 teaspoonful of Tournade's Kitchen Bouquet and send in a sauce bowl along with the roast turkey.

BOILED TURKEY.

Cut the legs at the first joint and draw them into the body. Fasten the small ends of the wings under the back and tie with twine. Sprinkle over it salt, pepper and lemon juice, put in boiling water and boil two hours. Serve in a bed of rice with oyster or caper sauce. Pour some of the sauce over the turkey.

BONED TURKEY

Boil in as little water as possible, until the bones can be

Use Mansfield's Pure Herbs

separated from the meat. Remove the skin, slice and mix the light and dark parts, season with pepper and salt. Boil down the liquor in which it was boiled and pour on the meat. Shape like a loaf of bread, wrap in a tight cloth and press with a heavy weight for a few hours. When served cut in thin slices.

ROAST GOOSE.

The goose should be young. Green geese are best when four months old. Skewer the legs and wings securely, stuff it and sprinkle the top with salt, pepper and flour; keep the giblets to boil and chop for gravy as you would turkey. Baste often. If it is green, roast an hour and a half, if old, bake in a pan with plenty of hot water; bake three or four hours. Serve with apple sauce.

ROAST DUCK.

Prepare the same as a goose. If they are ducklings roast thirty minutes. Full grown ducks should be roasted an hour and basted often. Serve with them giblet gravy or apple sauce.

Wild ducks should be cooked rare, with or without stuffing. Baste them first with hot water, to which add an onion and salt, then baste with butter and a little flour. Cook from twenty to thirty minutes. Serve with currant jelly.

DUCKS A LA FRANCAISE

Put two dozen chestnuts roasted and peeled into a pint of good gravy, with a sprig of thyme, two small onions, a few whole peppers, and a bit of ginger. Take a duck, lard the chest with shreds of bacon, and half roast it, then put it into the gravy, add a quarter of a pint of port wine, and let it stew about twenty minutes. When the duck is sufficiently done, take it out, boil up the gravy to a proper thickness, skim it clear of any fat add 1-2 teaspoonful of Tournade's Kitchen Bouquet, lay the duck in a dish, and pour the sauce over it.

BAKED SPRING CHICKENS.

Cut them open at the back; spread out in a pan and sprinkle with pepper, salt, flour and some water. Baste often,

Use Tournade's Kitchen Bouquet

and once or twice with butter. When done, rub butter over them and set in the oven a little while before serving.

CHICKEN FRICASSEE.

Boil forty minutes in water enough to cover them. Put part of the water in which they were boiled in a stewpan. For two chickens rub butter the size of an egg and a spoonful of flour together, and stir into the water. When it boils, add salt and one gill of milk. Lay in the chickens; cover the pan and stew twenty minutes.

CHICKEN TOAST.

Cut from the bones whatever meat can be readily removed, and chop it almost as fine as mince meat. Simmer the bones and trimmings (all skin and gristle must be rejected from the juice) for at least an hour, and strain off the resulting broth. To a cupful of this stock add a cupful of milk or sweet cream, two well beaten eggs and a pinch of salt. Use a little of it to moisten the minced chicken and set that on in a small saucepan to heat. Cut half a dozen thick slices from a loaf of bread, place them in a deep basin and pour the sauce over them. When they have absorbed as much as they will take up, fry quickly in a little fresh butter. Spread each slice thinly with the chicken. Good either hot or cold.

SMOTHERED CHICKEN

is particularly nice when the fowl is young and tender. Split the chicken down the back, cover it over with lumps of butter and pepper and salt; add one-half of a pint of water; cover closely and cook in the oven till done.

PRESSED CHICKEN.

Boil two chickens in water enough to cover them until the meat will drop from the bones. Then pick from the bones and season with salt and pepper. Put first a layer of dark and then a layer of white meat. Boil the water away to about half of a teacupful, and pour over the chicken. Put away to press, and let it stand over night before serving.

FRIED CHICKEN.

Take two chickens and cut in pieces. Sprinkle pepper

Headquarters for Fine Vermont Butter

and salt and let them stand one hour. Rub with flour before frying. Beat two eggs; dip each piece in this and fry in hot lard. Boil one and one-half cups of milk; add a spoonful of butter rubbed in a spoonful of flour and a little salt. Stir until it boils again. Lay chicken in a dish; pour the sauce around it and serve.

CHICKEN POT PIE.

Cut the chicken, put into boiling water and cook until tender. Chop the giblets and put into the broth. Season with pepper and salt. To each quart stir in two spoonfuls of flour mixed with cream. Break open, butter and throw in warm light biscuits. Cover tightly and simmer twenty minutes.

CHICKEN POT PIE.

Joint the chicken and parboil it. Make a crust the same as for soda biscuit, line the sides of the pot (not the bottom) with this; with the chicken lay in thin sliced potatoes, sprinkle in a little pepper, add salt and a bit of mace. If there was not broth enough left after parboiling the chicken, add water sufficient to cover the chicken when put in the pot; over the whole lay a piece of crust about the thickness of soda biscuit. Fold a towel and put over the pot, and put on the cover. The towel will hold the steam which rises, and prevent its falling back upon the crust to make it heavy. Before putting in the broth it should be thickened a little, and a little butter added.

DRESSING FOR MEAT AND POULTRY.

STUFFING FOR TURKEY, CHICKEN, VEAL, AND LAMB.—Soak one-half pound of bread, with the crust off, in tepid water, squeeze it dry; put three ounces of butter into a stewpan, when hot add one small onion minced, color slightly, then add the bread with three tablespoonfuls of parsley chopped fine, one-half teacupful powdered thyme, pepper and salt.

STUFFING FOR ROAST TURKEY, CHICKEN, DUCK AND GOOSE.—Two onions, five ounces soaked and squeezed bread, eight sage leaves, one ounce butter, pepper, salt, one egg. Mince the onions and fry in the pan before adding the other ingredients.

Potted Meats and Poultry always in stock

 # FRY'S English Chocolate and Cocoa.

PURE,

NUTRITIOUS,   **ECONOMICAL.**

Crosse & Blackwell's

London Fresh Fruit Preserves, Jams, Orange Marmalade, Chow-chow, Mixed and other Pickles in pure Malt Vinegar, Currie Powder, China Soy, Parmasan Cheese, Anchovy Paste.

S. Rae's
PURE OLIVE OIL,

For Salads,

Is prepared from the most perfectly ripened and selected Olives of Tuscany.

The above Choice Table Articles Sold by W. H. Mansfield & Co.

Tarbox's
STOVE GLOSS!

Black your Stove Twice a Year, the Top Once a Week, and always have a nice looking stove.

A light brushing will renew the polish whenever it looks dull. It will pay you to give it a trial.

———— MANUFACTURED BY ————

The Tarbox Manufg. Company,

NEW LONDON, CONN.

———— FOR SALE BY ————

W. H. MANSFIELD & CO.,

Putnam, Conn.

MEATS.

CORNED BEEF

should be put into hot water to boil. When boiling ham or corned beef put in two tablespoons of vinegar to give a good color.

Spring is the best season for mutton; that which is not very large is to be preferred. It should be of a good red and white, and fine grain.

LAMB

is best in July and August. Veal is best in spring. It should look white and be fat. The breast is particularly nice stuffed. The loin should be roasted.

BEEFSTEAK.

Porter House and tenderloin are best. Grease the gridiron. Have it hot. Put your steak over a hot fire, cover with a baking pan, turn as soon as colored, watch constantly and turn again as soon as browned. It should be quite rare or pink in the center. Put on a hot platter, sprinkle with pepper and salt, spread butter over it and serve immediately. There should be no gravy. Lemon juice and chopped parsley added before the butter improves it.

HINTS ABOUT BOILING MEATS.

All kinds of meat intended for the table should be put into boiling water, thereby retaining the juices. If it is desired to give a salt flavoring to them, boil a piece of salt pork in the water before putting the meat in. A nice piece of boiled salt pork is a great addition to all kinds of boiled meats. Corned, salt or smoked meats should be put into cold water to cook. Great care should be taken to skim the scum off well just before the water boils; for if the scum boils into the water, it is impossible to take it off, and it will adhere to the meats.

Capers, Olives, Olive Oil, Table Sauces

TO MAKE THE IRISH STEW.

One of the most inexpensive, palatable and wholesome dishes is the Irish stew. About two pounds of the neck of mutton, four onions, six large potatoes, salt, pepper, three pints of water and two tablespoonfuls of flour. Cut the mutton in handsome pieces. Put about half the fat in the stewpan, with the onions, and stir for eight or ten minutes over a hot fire; then put in the meat, which sprinkle with the flour, salt and pepper. Stir ten minutes, and add the water, boiling. Set for one hour where it will simmer; then add the potatoes, peeled and cut in quarters. Simmer an hour longer and serve. You can cook dumplings with this dish, if you choose. They are a great addition to all kinds of stews and ragouts.

BAKED HAM.

Take a medium-sized ham and soak twenty-four hours in cold water; wipe and scrape clean; make rather a stiff paste of rye meal and water, cover the ham entirely with the paste and bake in a moderate oven six hours. This is much nicer than boiled ham.

ROAST PORK.

Stuff the spare-rib with sage dressing, allow twenty minutes for each pound, baste it with butter first; after that with its own drippings. Apple sauce is served with it.

BOILED HAM.

Put the ham into a pot of cold water; let it simmer slowly eight hours; leave in the water until cold; then peel off the skin.

HAM AND EGGS.

Ham should be fried in its own fat, well done. Take out of the spider, add lard, break the eggs one at a time, in a cup, put them in the fat and baste.

VEAL CHOPS.

Roll them in bread crumbs and fry in hot pork fat; fringed white paper around the ribs adds very much to their looks.

Use Mansfield's Pure Herbs and Spices

MUTTON.

The best roasts are the leg, the saddle, and the shoulder of mutton. To boil it, put into salted, boiling water and do not let it stop boiling until done. Boil one-quarter of an hour for each pound. Caper sauce should be served with it.

LAMB.

The best roasts are the fore and hind quarters. Roast lamb should be well done on the outside and pink within; it must be served hot, with caper or mint sauce. A fore-quarter of lamb should be stuffed with a veal stuffing. It should be well seasoned with pepper and salt, and basted often.

ROAST BEEF.

To be properly roasted the meat should be placed on an iron rack in the pan, dusted over with flour and salt, then placed in a quick oven to brown the outside and retain the juices. After it has been well browned add a quart of water beneath the meat, place an onion in the water and let the meat cook slowly for an hour and a half. Just before taking the meat from the oven, make a paste of flour and water, mixing carefully to avoid lumps. Take the meat from the pan, remove the onion, and set the pan upon the stove. While the water is boiling add the paste gradually, stirring constantly until the gravy is of the right consistency. Salt and pepper to suit the taste.

BOILED HAM.

Scrape the ham and wash it clean. Place it in hot water and add one-half cup of sugar, one onion, one-half teaspoon of pepper. Boil all day. When done the meat will draw away from the bone. With a sharp knife cut off the rind and part of the fat, and place the ham in a baking pan. Pound together one-half cup of sugar and sprinkle over the ham. Stick in whole cloves and brown well in the oven.

DRESSING FOR HAM SANDWICHES.

Two spoonfuls of cream, one of Rae's olive oil, yolks of two eggs, sugar, mustard to taste.

Pitted Olives, quite a novelty, and very nice

ROAST BEEF.

Wipe the meat with a wet towel and dredge on all sides with flour. Have a rack that will fit loosely in the baking pan. Cover the bottom of the pan lightly with flour; put in rack and then meat. Place in a very hot oven for a few minutes to brown the flour; add hot water enough to cover the bottom of the pan. In ten minutes baste with the gravy, dredge with salt, pepper and flour. Do this every fifteen minutes. Brown one side, then turn and brown the other.

YORKSHIRE PUDDING.

Six eggs, six tablespoons of flour, one pint of milk. Beat to a smooth batter and bake in dripping-pan under roast beef, half an hour before the beef is done. Serve with the meat.

SCALLOPED ROAST BEEF.

Cut roast beef in small pieces and put one layer in bottom of pudding dish, add one layer of chopped onion, bread broken in small pieces, and gravy. So on until the dish is full, the last layer of onion and bread crumbs. Serve hot.

POT PIE OF VEAL OR BEEF.

One-quarter pound of pork fried out in a sauce-pan; take out the scraps, add meat and brown it, add raw potatoes sliced, pepper and salt; cover this with water; let it cook one hour; add a rich paste crust.

TO BAKE VEAL.

Fill it with stuffing made of two cupfuls of bread crumbs, one-half cupful of chopped pork, one-half lemon peel grated, a little juice, also summer savory. Bind the veal into a round form, fasten it with skewers, sprinkle pepper and salt over it and cover with buttered paper. Baste well and often. Just before it is done sprinkle with flour and rub butter on it. Bake three hours.

STEWED KIDNEYS.

Cut them in thin round slices. Cover with cold water; let them stand twenty minutes; put them in a stew-pan with one quart of water or stock, a clove, one tablespoonful of on-

Always Use the Celebrated Victor Flour

ion juice, salt and pepper. Simmer two hours. Put one tablespoonful of butter in a pan, add one of flour. Stir until brown and smooth; add the kidneys.

A NICE WAY TO USE UP REMNANTS OF MEAT.

Having freed the meat from all bone and fat, chop very fine. Place in a sauce-pan and add a piece of butter, water enough to make the mass soft, and season with salt and pepper. While this is slowly heating, toast several slices of bread, place them over the surface of a heated platter. Moisten each slice of bread with a little hot water and spread upon them the minced meat. Serve hot. This makes a good breakfast dish.

FINGER SANDWICHES.

One tablespoon of butter, a little flour, a little salt, boiling milk enough to thicken, cook a little. Put by until thoroughly cold, then add chopped chicken, lobster or ham. Cut bread diamond shape and fill with the mixture.

MEAT PIE.

One pound of cold baked lamb, beef or veal, cut in small pieces, four raw potatoes sliced thin; first a layer of meat, then a layer of potatoes, pepper, salt and butter; fill a pudding dish in this way; at the top add cold gravy if you have it; also one beaten egg, and one-half pint of warm water; cover this with pie crust and bake one hour.

SECOND DAY OF ROAST BEEF.

Cut the beef into slices, removing most of the fat. Rub each slice in flour, place in layers in a covered earthern dish alternating with layers of fresh or can of Old Reliable tomatoes, sprinkling each layer with pepper, salt, summer savory, and sweet marjoram—curry powder if you like it. Turn cold gravy over the top with just enough water to cover the meat. Add two or three whole cloves. Bake three or four hours, adding flour if the gravy is not thick enough. About twenty minutes before serving remove the cover and brown.

BEEF LOAF No. 1.

Three pounds of raw beef chopped fine, six crackers

Old Reliable Soap is Strictly Pure

rolled fine, two eggs, two cups milk, one tablespoonful of salt, one teaspoonful of pepper; bake one and one-half hours.

BEEF LOAF No. 2.

Take two pounds of lean beef, chopped fine, three eggs, four soda crackers rolled, salt and pepper to taste, and one teaspoonful of butter. Make into a loaf and bake, baste occasionally with butter and water.

SHIN BONE LOAF.

Take a shin bone (beef) and boil till you can remove from the bone easily, then chop fine and season to taste with salt, pepper and sage; pour over it some of the water (while warm) in which the meat was boiled, and have ready hard boiled eggs to place lengthwise through the center of loaf. Put in a pan and press.

VEAL LOAF.

Four pounds of lean veal, one pound of fat salt pork, chopped fine before cooking, to which add four eggs, two cups of cracker crumbs (rolled fine), one cup of water, salt, pepper and sage to taste. Bake in slow oven three hours. Butter may be used instead of pork.

BAKED CHOPS.

Cut into slices, the thickness of a penny, raw potatoes; arrange in a baking dish and sprinkle each layer with salt and pepper; put in enough cold water to prevent burning. Place the dish on the top shelf of a very hot oven in order to brown the potatoes in a few minutes. Have ready some loin chops, (one for each person). When the potatoes are browned remove the dish from the oven and place the chops on the top, add a little salt, pepper, and hot water if required. Cook about three-quarters of an hour.

HASHED MEAT BALLS.

One cup of chopped remnants of steak or any meat, two cups of chopped boiled potatoes, pepper and salt, butter half size of an egg. Shape into round cakes by taking flour into the hand. Fry in butter.

Old Reliable Soap is Harmless

HARICOT OF MUTTON.

Divide the chops of a two pound loin of mutton, take off the superfluous fat, cut two onions into rings, and fry them with the meat a nice brown, in a good sized piece of butter, thicken a half pint of gravy with a little flour, and pour it over the chops. Set them at the side of the fire to stew slowly for three-quarters of an hour, or rather more. Parboil two carrots, two turnips, and half a head of celery, cut the former into shapes, and the celery into slices, and add them to the meat about twenty minutes before serving. Pour in a glass of port wine, two spoonfuls of catsup, a little Tournade's Kitchen Bouquet, and after boiling it once up, serve it hot.

OLD RELIABLE SOAP

———FOR THE———

Laundry, Kitchen, Bath Room,

And General Cleaning Purposes.

Will not injure the finest fabric.

Will not harm the skin.

Made of choicest materials, and contains no rosin or any injurious article.

Most economical Soap in the market.

W. H. Mansfield & Co.,

Sole Proprietors.

Rockwood & Co's

Cocoas and Chocolates

We heartily recommend to our customers.

W. H. Mansfield & Co.

Try Acorn Brand Chocolate Creams

DRINK
O. & O. TEA

The finest Imported.   Blended from

The Choicest Grades of Leaf

After years of study by skilled experts.

One trial will satisfy you that it is superior to any other Tea on offer, and is at the same time more economical than the lower grades, as it takes less of it to make Tea of the desired strength.

———FOR SALE BY———

W. H. MANSFIELD & CO., Putnam

VEGETABLES.

Always let the water boil before putting in the vegetables, and continue to do so until they are done.

TURNIPS.

Turnips should be pealed and boiled from forty minutes to an hour.

BEETS.

Beets should be boiled from one to two hours, then put in cold water and slip off the skins.

SPINACH.

Boil twenty minutes.

POTATO PUFFS.

Boil and mash the potatoes, salt and pepper, make into balls; while hot, brush over the balls with the beaten yolk of an egg. Butter a tin pan, brown them quickly in a hot oven from five to ten minutes.

POTATO CHIPS.

Slice potatoes very thin with slicer or sharp knife, soak in cold water from ten to twenty-four hours to remove the starch, and fry in hot fat until brown. Drain upon brown paper, and sprinkle with salt while still warm. The frying basket must not be more than one-third full at a time, and must be held so as to be easily lifted from the fat should there be any danger of its boiling over before the water evaporates. The potatoes can be fried the day before using if more convenient, as they can easily be recrisped by placing a few moments in the oven.

STEWED POTATOES.

One-half pint of milk; let it come to a boil, add butter, pepper, salt and flour enough to thicken, dissolved in cold water. Lastly put in four large boiled potatoes cut in squares. Heat thoroughly.

SCALLOPED POTATOES.

Cut six boiled potatoes in small pieces. Make a dressing of one pint of milk and three spoons of flour. Boil until

Buy your Potatoes of Us

it thickens; add piece of butter the size of an egg, salt and pepper enough to make it very hot. Put into a pudding dish alternate layers of potatoes and dressing, and over the top a layer of bread crumbs. Put small bits of butter on top and bake half an hour.

MASHED POTATOES.

When boiled pour into a dish, which place over the fire. To half a cupful of milk, a piece of butter size of an egg, salt and pepper—let them get hot—add seven potatoes the moment they are done and mash without stopping until they are cool.

BAKED POTATOES WITH BEEF.

Pare potatoes of equal size and put them into the same pan in which the beef is baked. Every time the beef is basted the potatoes should be basted. Serve around the beef.

BRISTLED POTATOES.

Cut small boiled potatoes in two, place in a pan, add butter, pepper and salt, and brown in the oven.

LYONNAISE POTATOES.

One-half pound of cold boiled potatoes, two ounces of onions, a heaping teaspoonful of chipped parsley, butter size of an egg. Slice the potatoes, put the butter into a pan, add the onions (minced), fry to a light brown, then add parsley and serve hot.

PARSNIPS.

Boil from twenty or thirty minutes, until quite tender. Then slice and fry in hot fat.

ONIONS.

Boil onions in two waters. Add milk the last time.

STRING BEANS.

String beans should be carefully strung and cut in small pieces. Boil one hour. Season with salt, pepper and butter.

SHELLED BEAS.

Boil from half to one hour.

GREEN CORN.

Boil half an hour.

Best Butter and Cheese at Mansfield's

GREEN PEAS.

Peas should not be shelled until just before they are cooked, and they should not be washed, as it takes the sweetness from them. Put into boiling salted water and boil briskly for twenty-five minutes.

BAKED TOMATOES.

Do not skin them. Scoop out a place in the tops and fill with dressing made of one onion fried in butter, add bread crumbs moistened with water, and season with cayenne pepper and salt. Fry them a moment; fill with the stuffing; let it project over the tops and smooth it down. Bake.

ONIONS WITH CREAM.

Boil them in salted water with a little milk until tender. Drain and put them in a stewpan with a white sauce made as directed for cauliflower. Serve with the sauce poured over them.

LIMA BEANS WITH CREAM.

One pint of beans into enough salted water to cover them. When tender drain off the water, add one cupful of boiling milk; butter, pepper and salt. Let them simmer in the milk before serving.

CAULIFLOWER WITH SAUCE.

Boil the cauliflower until tender in well salted water. Put pieces of butter size of an egg into a pan; when it bubbles, stir in half a cupful of flour; add two cups of milk; pepper and salt. Stir all together over the fire until smooth. Pour the sauce over the cauliflower.

ASPARAGUS.

Tie the stalks in bunches with the heads all one way. Boil in salted water twenty minutes. Prepare thin slices of toast. Drain the asparagus, lay it on the toast, pour over it.

ASPARAGUS DRESSING.

Melt butter the size of an egg in the spider, put in gradually about a dessertspoonful of flour. Add one cup of cream; pepper and salt to taste. Cook about eight minutes.

Best Brands of Macaroni, Vermicelli, etc.

MACARONI.

Take half a pound of macaroni and stew in a saucepan of boiling water slightly salted, until soft and tender. When drained, put a layer in a baking-dish, and grate over it a layer of cheese, adding bits of butter. Put layer upon layer until the dish is filled, finishing with a layer of cheese and a half cup of milk. Bake covered half an hour, then brown and serve in same dish.

STRING BEANS.

This delicious vegetable is rarely properly cooked. When well prepared it is quite as healthful as peas. Take the pods as fresh and young as possible, and shred them as finely as a small knife will go through them, cutting them lengthwise, and, as it were, shaving them very thin. Put into salted boiling water and boil two hours. Then drain in a colander and serve with plenty of sweet butter, and they will be as delicate as peas. If one likes vinegar a little of it will improve the dish.

STEWED TOMATOES.

Take six tomatoes, pour boiling water over them so as to remove the skin; put them in a saucepan. Add butter, pepper and salt. Let them cook fifteen minutes. Bread crumbs may be added.

CABBAGE

Should be boiled nearly or quite an hour in plenty of water. Salt while boiling.

CORN FRITTERS.

Put one can of Old Reliable Corn into a bowl with two eggs well beaten, half a teaspoonful of salt, a pinch cayenne pepper, half pint milk, two ounces of melted butter and enough sifted flour to make a stiff batter. Drop spoonfuls of this in smoking hot fat and fry same as doughnuts.

GATEAU AU RIZ.

Sufficient boiled rice to fill a mould, two eggs beaten, extract of vanilla, bread crumbs. Steam the rice. Salt it well. Do not stir it but shake the pan gently. When it is

Largest Stock of Farinaceous Goods in the County

nearly done, add rice and milk and let it steam until the milk is absorbed sufficiently. When it is done, add the beaten egg and flavoring. Butter a mould. Strew bread crumbs in the bottom of it. Put in the rice and bake one-half hour. Turn it out of the mould. Serve hot.

TO FRY APPLES.

Wash and wipe six large, fair, juicy apples that are not too tart; remove cores with a sharp knife or apple corer; cut the apple around in slices half an inch thick; fry in hot butter until the slices are nicely browned on both sides; sprinkle with powdered sugar after removing to the dish in which they are to be served. A nice accompaniment for roast pork.

TO MAKE CRANBERRY SAUCE.

Wash and pick a quart of cranberries and put them into a saucepan with a teacupful of water; stew slowly, stirring often until they are as thick as marmalade; they require at least one hour and a half to cook; when you take them from the fire sweeten them abundantly with white sugar; if sweetened while cooking the color will be dark; put into a mould and set aside to get cold.

TO BOIL APPLES.

Place a layer of fair-skinned Baldwins--or any nice variety—in the stewpan, with about a quarter of an inch of water. Throw on about one-half cup sugar to six good-sized apples, and boil until the apples are thoroughly cooked and the syrup nearly thick enough for jelly. After one trial no one would, for any consideration, have fair-skinned apples peeled. The skins contain a very large share of the pictous --jelly-making—substances, and impart a flavor impossible to obtain otherwise. A wise housekeeper, instead of throwing away the skins and cores of sound pie apples would use them for jelly. A tumblerful of the richest sort can thus be obtained from a dozen apples. Boil the skins, etc., a few minutes, and strain. Add a little sugar to the liquid, and boil until right to turn into the tumbler.

Don't fail to use Mansfield's Extracts

TO BAKE BEANS.

Parboil three cups of beans; turn off the water and put in a beanpot with one pound of pork, streaked with lean. First cut the pork rind in gashes and put in pepper and mustard. Nearly cover with water and cook slowly six or eight hours.

RICE CROQUETTES.

Three pints of milk, one cup of rice, one teaspoonful of salt; cook three hours in double boiler. Beat to a paste and stir in two eggs, two teaspoonfuls of vanilla, a piece of butter size of an egg, two tablespoonfuls of sugar. To serve as a dessert, take half the weight and put in small pudding dish, beat whites of two eggs to stiff froth, add one teaspoon lemon juice, and sift over top of Meringue, one teaspoon of powdered sugar, and brown. Serve with fancy sauce or cream. For croquettes cool the remainder, form into oblong balls put in wire baskets and fry in beef suet. Beef suet is better than any other fat for frying croquettes. Serve croquettes with pieces of jelly on each.

CHICKEN CROQUETTES.

One-half pound chicken, chopped fine; season with one-half teaspoon salt, one-half teaspoon celery salt, one-fourth salt-spoon of cayenne pepper, one teaspoon white pepper, a few drops onion juice, one teaspoon chopped parsley, one teaspoon lemon juice. Make one pint of very thick cream sauce and mix with the chicken. Shape in the hand and roll first in cracker crumbs, then in the yolk of an egg. Fry in beef suet.

BAKED EGGS.

Break as many eggs as you wish into a buttered dish, nearly cover them with milk, add several small pieces of butter and sprinkle with pepper. Bake a few minutes till the white has set.

STUFFED EGGS.

Remove the shells from hard boiled eggs, cut carefully lengthwise and remove yolks. Mash the yolks thoroughly, season with butter, pepper, salt and chopped cucumber

Fresh Country Eggs always on hand

pickle. Fill the cavities and put the halves together, then roll each egg in white tissue paper, twisting it at the ends.

OMELET.

Four eggs and four tablespoons of milk. Beat the whites separately to a stiff froth, stir in lightly the yolks which have been beaten with the milk and salt, pour into a hot buttered spider, and brown lightly. Place in the oven long enough to stiffen but not brown the top, fold and serve immediately.

BREAD CRUMB OMELET.

One cup of bread crumbs, one cup of hot milk beaten with the crumbs, yolks of four eggs, one tablespoonful of melted butter, whites of four eggs beaten stiff, stir in the last thing.

PLAIN OMELET.

Beat, very thoroughly, the yolks of five eggs, one dessert spoon of flour rubbed smooth in two-thirds of a cup of milk, salt and pepper to taste, and a piece of butter as large as a walnut.

POACHED EGGS.

Boil a pint of milk. While boiling beat six eggs to a froth. Just before the milk begins to boil, add half a tablespoonful of butter and a teaspoonful of salt, and stir into it; then pour in the eggs, stir without ceasing, but gently, till it thickens—not more than two minutes. Take it from the stove or range, and continue to stir half a minute or so, and then pour it over two or three thin slices of toasted bread, which has been spread with butter, and all prepared in a deep dish before the eggs are put into the milk. This is very nice for breakfast.

HARD SCRABBLED.

Put two teaspoonfuls of butter into a frying pan. Beat six eggs. Season with pepper and salt. When the butter is very hot, but not scorched, put in the eggs; stir until it thickens, and serve hot.

HAM AND EGG TOAST.

Toast slices of bread. Butter and spread with cold ham,

Use Mansfield's Spices in Salads

chopped and seasoned. Drop an egg in boiling, salted water until the white is set, then put on top of ham. A delicious breakfast dish

HAM OMELET.

Chopped boiled ham (one cupful), four eggs well beaten, one-half cup milk, one teaspoonful melted butter; butter a flat pan, pour in the mixture, and cook like any omelet.

TOMATO OMELET.

Chop fine one can of Old Reliable tomatoes, two chopped onions, a little butter, salt and pepper, one cracker pounded fine; cover tight and let simmer an hour. Beat five eggs to a froth, have a hot griddle and pour the eggs into the tomato. Brown on one side, fold, brown on the other.

EGG SANDWICHES.

Chop while hot hard boiled eggs, add butter, pepper and salt. Cut crust from bread and spread mixture between.

SALAD DRESSING NO. 1.

One tablespoonful of mustard, one teaspoonful of sguar (scant), one-tenth of a tea-poonful of cayenne pepper one teaspoonful of salt, juice of half a lemon, one-qurter of a cup of vinegar, yolks of three uncooked eggs, yolk of three cooked eggs, one pint of Rae's Olive oil. Beat the yolks and dry the ingredients together until very light and thick. Add a few drops of oil at a time until the dressing becomes hard; when it becomes to thick to beat, add a little of the lemon, stir more oil, and so on until it is used up.

SALAD DRESSING NO. 2.

One teaspoon of salt, one of pepper, one of dry mustard, two tablespoons of sugar dissolved in a little hot water, three tablespoons of melted butter, three well beaten eggs, two-thirds of a cup of vinegar, one cup of cream. Mix and cook until thick as cream.

SALAD DRESSING NO. 3.

Yolks of eight eggs well beaten, one tablespoon of sugar, one-half cup of cream, one cup of butter, three tablespoons of ground mustard, one-half teaspoon of cayenne pepper,

Best brands of Salad preparations

one pint of vinegar; cook in water to the consistency of custard. Bottle tight. It will keep one year.

SALAD DRESSING NO. 4.

Four tablespoonfuls of butter, one tablespoonful of flour, one tablespoonful of salt, one tablespoonful of sugar, one heaping teaspoonful of mustard, a speck of cayenne, one cupful of milk, one-half cupful of vinegar, three eggs. Let the butter get hot in a saucepan, add the flour and stir until smooth, being careful not to brown; add the milk and boil; place the saucepan in a dish of hot water: beat the eggs, salt, pepper, sugar and mustard together, add the vinegar, stir this into the boiling mixture until it thickens like soft custard, which will be about five minutes. Set away to cool; when cold bottle, and place in ice chest. This will keep two weeks.

SALAD DRESSING NO. 5.

Yolk of one egg, put it in a soup plate; add the oil drop by drop, stiring all one way with a silver fork until it is as thick as the beaten white of an egg when dropped from the fork. Add half a teaspoonful at a time of lemon juice, alternately with a teaspoonful of oil; thin it in this way until like soft custard. Make two plates full for a salad; one mix with the meat, the other spread over the top. This dressing should be used for chicken, shrimp, lobster and potatoes salad.

CHICKEN SALAD—MIRAND.

Put one quart of chicken in a bowl with three tablespoonfuls of vinegar, one tablespoonful of Rae's Olive oil, one large teaspoonful of salt, and one-half teaspoonful of pepper. Let it stand one hour.

CHICKEN SALAD.

One chicken (cut in small squares); let it stand as directed in the Mirand. Half a bunch of celery chopped fine, let it stand until cold and crisp in ice water. Mix chicken and celery together, add one plate of salad dressing. Place on a platter, dress around the edge with celery tips; spread one plateful of salad dressing over the top of the chicken.

Be wise and use Victor Flour

Put a row of olives around it, and boiled eggs cut in rings or beets cut in pointed pieces. Lobster salad is made the same way only add mustard and curry powder with seasoning. Dress platter with lettuce, omit olives.

POTATO SALAD NO. 1.

One quarts of boiled potatoes cut in thin slices, then in small squares, while warm, not hot; one tablespoonful of grated onion, two tablespoons of chopped parsley, and enough of the "cream salad dressing" to make moist. Put in a cool place for an hour or two.

CREAM SALAD DRESSING.

One teaspoonful of sugar, salt and mustard rubbed smoothly together, with one teaspoonful of Rae's oil; add three eggs well beaten, two-thirds of a cup of cream, and one-half cup of vinegar. Place within a kettle of boiling water and cook until it thickens.

POTATO SALAD NO. 2.

Boil a piece of butter size of a large egg in three-fourths of a cup of vinegar and one-fourth of a cup of water. Mix the yolks of two large eggs, or three small ones, juice and grated rind of one lemon, one teaspoon each of mustard, salt, curry powder (scant) and sugar, one-half teaspoon of pepper. Add all, well beaten, to the hot vinegar, also one-half cup of cream, rich milk or white of egg. Strain and set on stove to thicken. Boil eight potatoes with two or three sliced red beets, cut up salt and pepper. Grate the yolks of two hard boiled eggs and sprinkle over the dressing. Garnish with rounds of the boiled whites.

CABBAGE SALAD NO. 1.

One cup of vinegar scalded with butter size of an egg. Reserve part of the vinegar and mix with one and one half teaspoons of mustard, two eggs beaten, two teaspoons of sugar and one of salt. Beat all together and add to the scalding vinegar. For two pounds of cabbage.

CABBAGE SALAD NO. 1.

Yolks of two eggs well beaten, one teaspoons of salt and pepper, one tablespoonful of sugar, two of melted butter, four of vinegar, two of water. Let it come to a boil and pour over the chopped cabbage. Then stand until cold. A teaspoon of mustard may be added if liked.

LETTUCE SALAD.

Two heads of lettuce, two hard boiled eggs, two teaspoon of butter, one-half teaspoon of salt, one teaspoon of white sugar, one-half teaspoon made mustard, one teaspoon of pepper, four tablespoons of vinegar. Rub yolks of eggs to a powder, add sugar, butter, pepper, salt, mustard, let stand five minuaes, beat in vinegar.

SAUCE TARTARE.

Put into a very small bowl the yolks of two eggs, a dessert spoonful of the best vinegar, and a little salt; whip up this mixture with a whisk as quickly as possible. When the whole forms a sort of cream, add two dessert spoonfuls of oil, and a teaspoonful of mustard, which must be well mixed previously; a pinch of parsley minced very fine, and a little cayenne. The oil should be put in drop by drop to mix perfectly. A little of Tournade's Kitchen Bouquet improves the flavor.

—FOR MAKING—

MUSH, GEMS, PUDDINGS, &C.

FOULDS' WHEAT GERM MEAL

Purest,
Healthiest,
Best,
And most popular preparation of WHEAT On the Market.

Palatable,
Delicate,
Easily Digested
And very nourishing

Excellent for Invalids

COOKS IN FIVE MINUTES!

Highly recommended by

W. H. MANSFIELD & CO., Putnam

F. M. LEONARD,

BOSTON, MASS.,

Wholesale Dealer in

Foreign and Domestic Fruits

Sole New England Agent for

Bishop, Hoyt & Co's

ORANGE LAKE FLORIDA ORANGES

**A USEFUL PRESENT A DIFFERENT PRESENT
AN ACCEPTABLE PRESENT**

In every Package.

KING OF WASHING POWDERS.

I have used three of the principal Washing Powders now sold at the stores, and I have thoroughly tried Savena. It is certainly superior to any other Washing Powder. In my opinion it is the "King of Washing Powders," and just what housekeepers want. I can do my washing in just half the time, and with less hard labor, by using Savena. For all woolens, say blankets, flannels, underwear, etc., it has no equal. It thoroughly cleanses woolens with very little rubbing, leaving them soft and white, without shrinking, and without the least injury to the hands or clothes. Housekeepers, try it.—Mrs. G. T. Louger, Middletown, N. H.

BREAD.

WEIGHTS AND MEASURES

One quart flour weighs one pound.
One quart Indian meal weighs one pound two ounces.
One quart soft butter weighs one pound one ounce.
One quart lump sugar weighs one pound.
One quart powdered sugar weighs one pound one ounce.
One quart best brown sugar weighs one pound two ounces.
Ten eggs average one pound.
Two cups sifted flour weigh one pound.
One pint sifted flour weighs one pound.
One pint white sugar weighs one pound.
Two tablespoons of liquid weighs one ounce.
One gill weighs four ounces.
One pint weighs sixteen ounces.

YEAST BREAD, NOT KNEADED.

Scald one pint of milk and one cooking spoon of sugar. Cut a cooking spoonful of butter into what you think enough flour to make a soft batter, and add a scant spoonful of salt. Dissolve one-half a yeast cake in luke warm water. Add one pint of water to the milk, having the mixture luke warm, at least. Pour this on to the flour, turn in your dissolved yeast cake and stir. Add more flour if necessary until you have quite a stiff batter, though not as stiff as if you kneaded it. Cover and put in a warm place. In the morning cut it down with a knife and form into loaves, if possible not adding any dry flour.

BREAD.

One quart of milk well scalded, one-half yeast cake dissolved in luke warm water or milk. When the milk is cool, add two tablespoons of sugar and one teaspoon of salt. Pour upon about two quarts of flour, if necessary add more flour

The Victor Fancy Patent is the Best

to make a stiff batter. This is not to be moulded but stirred with a spoon. In the morning add two tablespoons of melted butter. Knead half an hour and let it rise a very little, then put in pans and let it rise about one-third of what you wish when baked. Bake in a moderate oven. Bake slowly twenty minutes, browning a little, then cover with paper and bake about forty minutes.

TO MAKE PARKER HOUSE ROLLS.

Two quarts of flour, make a hole in the middle and put in one-half cup of sifted white sugar, lard size of one half an egg, one pint cold boiled milk, a little salt, one teacup good yeast; let it stand over night without kneading; in the morning stir it up, place it on the board and knead it well fifteen minutes, then put it in the pan again and let rise in a cold place till noon; about two hours before baking, roll out pretty thin and cut out with a pint pail cover, put a little butter on one-half the top and double it over. Allow plenty of room in the pan for rising, and when light bake from ten to fifteen minutes.

BROWN BREAD No. 1.

Three cups of Indian meal, three cups of boiling water poured over the meal, add two cups of rye meal, one cup of molasses, one and one-half cups of sweet milk, one teaspoon of salt, two large spoonfuls of soda dissolved in the milk. Steam four hours.

BROWN BREAD No. 2.

One cup of Indian meal with water enough to scald it, one cup of rye meal, one cup of sour milk with two teaspoons of soda stirred into it, one cup of sweet milk, one cup of molasses, one teaspoon of salt, one tablespoon butter, one egg if you choose, two dozen raisins to flavor, flour to thicken, mix soft.

BROWN BREAD No. 3.

One pint of Indian meal, one pint of rye meal, one cup of flour, one cup of molasses, one quart of buttermilk, one teaspoonful of soda, one teaspoonful of salt.

All kinds of Selected Corn Meals

BROWN BREAD No. 4.

Three cups of Indian meal, one cup of flour, two cups of sweet milk, one cup of sour milk, one cup of molasses; soda and salt. Steam four hours.

BROWN BREAD No. 5.

Two pints of rye, one pint of Indian meal, one cup of molasses, one pint of buttermilk with two teaspoons of soda dissolved in it. Mix with enough sweet milk or water to make a thick batter. Add a dessert spoon of salt. Steam five or six hours.

BUNNS.

Three cups of warm milk, one and one-half cups of sugar, one-half cup of yeast (or one-half yeast cake dissolved in water), flour enough for batter. In the morning, when very light, add one and one-half cups of sugar, one-half cup of melted butter and one teaspoon of cinnamon. Knead stiff and let it rise again, then cut into bits and add raisins, four or five to each bunn. Let it rise again in pans, bake in a moderate oven, and while still hot moisten the tops with equal parts of milk and molasses.

HOT BISCUITS.

One quart of flour with one teaspoon of soda, and a little salt sifted into it; then work in one tablespoonful of butter, and mix with buttermilk or sour milk as soft as you can handle. Do not knead it, but cut out and bake the biscuits as quickly as possible, wetting the tops and sides with a little melted butter.

CORN CAKE No. 1.

Two-thirds of a cup of meal, one cup of flour, three tablespoons of melted butter and lard mixed, one cup of milk, one teaspoon of soda, one tablespoon of sugar, two teaspoons of cream tartar. Rub meal, flour, sugar, cream tartar and a little salt together. Add milk and soda.

CORN CAKE No. 2.

Two coffee cups of white corn flour, one coffee cup of flour, two coffee cups of milk, two-thirds of a coffee cup of sugar, one-half coffee cup of butter, two eggs, two teaspoonfuls Royal Baking Powder.

Fancy Molasses we brag about

CORN MEAL BREAD No. 3.

One cup of meal, one of flour, one of milk, one egg, one-half cup of sugar, two teaspoonfuls of cream tartar, one of soda and one of salt.

WHEAT MUFFINS.

One quart of flour, two cups of sweet milk, two eggs, two teaspoonfuls of Royal Baking Powder, one-half teaspoonful of salt, butter the size of an egg. Mix the dry ingredients with the flour and rub through a sieve; melt the butter with four tablespoonfuls of boiling water; beat the eggs light and add the milk; stir into the flour and add the butter; beat thoroughly. Bake in buttered muffin pans twenty-five to thirty minutes in a quick oven. One-half quantity may be used as well.

BUCKWHEAT CAKES.

One quart of buckwheat flour, one teaspoon of salt, stir in water to make a thin batter and beat thoroughly, then four tablespoons of yeast, set in a warm place and rise over night. In the morning add one teaspoon of soda, also two tablespoons of molasses.

CORN GRIDDLE CAKES.

Add half a pint of milk to one can Old Reliable Corn; beat same; beat up two eggs in a bowl, add one teaspoonful sugar, two saltspoonfuls of salt dissolved in a gill of water, five tablespoonfuls of flour, and ten tablespoonfuls of the corn, mix well; this makes a thick batter. Just before using stir in a teaspoonful of baking powder; use only one tablespoonful of the batter to each cake.

GRAHAM FRITTERS.

Two cups of sour milk or buttermilk; two cups of graham flour, six tablespoonfuls white flour, two tablespoonfuls sugar, one heaping teaspoonful soda, a little salt.

FRITTERS.

Two cups of sour milk, two eggs, two teaspoonfuls of soda, flour enough for a thin batter.

We sell only Pure Cream Tartar

APPLE FRITTERS.

Beat to a froth two eggs, and stir into this half a pint of milk, one teaspoonful of salt, two cups of flour; pare and core nice tart apples, cut in slices, dip them in the batter, being sure to have the apple well covered, and fry in boiling lard a delicate brown; sprinkle with sugar or dissolve any kind of jelly in a little hot water and pour over the fritters.

RYE BREAD.

Two cups of rye meal, four cups of flour, one-half cup of yeast, one tablespoonful of sugar, one hot mashed potato, one teaspoonful of soda, salt. Mix with warm water.

SQUASH BISCUITS.

Sift squash as for pies, and to a pint put one quart raised dough, add two tablespoons of butter and one of sugar. Beat thoroughly and set to rise. Put sugar and water on top after they are baked.

CREAM TARTAR BISCUITS.

Two cups of sweet milk, piece of butter size of an egg, two large teaspoonfuls of cream tartar, one teaspoonful of soda, little salt. Have a hot oven. Mix soft.

BUTTERMILK BISCUITS.

One quart of flour, two teaspoons cream tartar, two teaspoons soda, one coffee cup of buttermilk, salt; mix soft.

GRAHAM CAKES.

Two eggs, one cup of sugar, one-half cup of molasses, two and one-half cups of flour, one teaspoon of soda, one cup of buttermilk, one teaspoon of all kinds of spice, butter size of an egg, one cup of raisins, stoned and chopped. Bake in gem pans.

EMMA'S GRAHAM BREAD.

Two cups of flour, one cup of graham meal, one-half pint of scalded milk into which put three large iron spoons of molasses and a little salt. Mix graham with flour, add the wetting while warm, lastly add one-third of a yeast cake disolved in luke warm water; add a little water if needed; rise

We Handle the Best Graham Flour

MUFFINS.

One cup of milk, one egg, two tablespoonfuls of sugar, one of melted butter, two teaspoonfuls cream of tartar, one of soda, flour to make a batter as thick as cup cake. Bake in a roll pan in a very quick oven.

GRAHAM MUFFINS.

One and one-half cups graham flour, one and one-half cups of flour, two cups of buttermilk, one egg, two tablespoons of sugar, one tablespoon of melted butter, one teaspoon of soda, salt.

SALLY LUNN.

One quart of flour, piece of butter size of egg, three tablespoons of sugar, two eggs, two cups of milk, two teaspoons of cream tartar, one teaspoon of soda, salt. Scatter cream tartar, salt and sugar into flour, add eggs, butter melted, and one cup of milk; dissolve soda in remaining cup, and stir all together steadily a few minutes. Bake in two round pans.

POPOVERS.

Two cups of milk, two even cups of flour, two eggs, one teaspoon of salt. Bake one-half hour.

OATMEAL.

Pour two cups of boiling water on one cup of Nudavene Flakes, add a scant teaspoonful of salt, and boil one hour in a double kettle. Serve with cream.

Stir one large cup of H. O. into a pint and a half of boiling water, salt to taste; boil from three to five minutes, stirring constantly, and serve hot or cold with milk, cream, sugar or syrup. Or fry in slices after cooling thoroughly, and serve with butter, sugar or syrup.

Try our Pure Maple Syrup

"I WANT SOME MORE."

"I want some more."—*Oliver Twist.*

This immortal remark of Oliver's was occasioned by the sly action of the cook in substituting H-O for the commoner brands of oatmeal. Taken at breakfast H-O acts as a natural system tonic, and aids largely in removing the evils of dyspepsia and indigestion. It costs more and is worth more than other oats.

The H-O Company.

—FOR SALE BY—

W. H. MANSFIELD & CO., Putnam, Ct.

HAVE HOT
Royal Milk Biscuit

At Every Meal.

Serve them hot, and you will find them of the most delicious flavor, and the most desirable of any biscuit manufactured.

DIRECTIONS.

Place in a hot oven, immediately before breakfast, dinner, lunch or tea, a sufficient number for the table, and when warmed through place upon table and use while hot.

CAUTION—Do not let them remain in oven long enough to burn.

Those who have tried them in this way will use no other kind of cracker. Each cracker is stamped "Parks & Savage Royal." There are none genuine without our name, as we are the only manufacturers of this celebrated Biscuit.

(Ask your grocer for them.)

PARKS & SAVAGE,

HARTFORD, CONN.

———— FOR SALE BY ————

W. H. MANSFIELD & CO.

CAKE.

A TEST FOR SPONGE CAKE.

Put a piece of white paper into the oven, close the door and open in five minutes. If the paper is a rich yellow, the oven is right; if a light yellow it is too cool; if a dark brown too hot. For pound cake it should color the paper light brown; for cup cake, the same or hotter; for molasses and and all thin roll cakes, the paper should be dark brown.

FRUIT CAKE.

One pound of butter, one pound of sugar, one pound of eggs, two pounds of currants, two pounds of raisins, one and one-quarter pounds of citron, one pound of flour, one cup of molasses, one teaspoonful of soda, one nutmeg, one tablespoonful of cloves, one tablespoonful of cinnamon, and a half teaspoonful of mace. This makes two large loaves. If too dry, moisten with a little strong coffee.

RIBBON CAKE.

Two and a half cups of sugar, one of butter, one of sweet milk, one teaspoon Royal Baking Powder, four cups of flour, four eggs. Reserve a third of this mixture, and bake the rest in two loaves of the same size. Add to the third reserved one cup of raisins, one-fourth pound of citron, one cup of currants, two tablespoons of molasses, one teaspoon each of all kinds of spice. Bake in tin same size as other loaves. Put the three loaves together with the white of an egg or jelly, placing the fruit leaf in the middle. Frost loaf.

JUMBLES.

One and a half cups of sugar, three-fourths of a cup of butter, three eggs; three tablespoons sweet milk, one heaping teaspoon Royal Baking Powder. Mix with sufficient flour to roll; roll and sprinkle with sugar and a little mace.

NEAPONITAN CAKE.

White cake: One cup of butter, two cups of sugar, one cup of milk, two cups of flour, one cup of corn starch; one teaspoon of soda, two teaspoons of cream tartar, whites of

Dried Fruits a Specialty.

seven eggs beaten stiff. Mix the corn starch and flour together.

Dark cake: One cup of butter, one cup of molasses, one cup of very strong coffee, two cups of brown sugar, four and one-half cups of flour, four eggs, one teaspoon of soda in the coffee, two teaspoons of cinnamon, cloves and mace, one and one-half pounds of currants, citron and raisins.

Filling and frosting: The whites of two eggs, juice of two lemons and grated rind of one, and powdered sugar enough to make a stiff frosting.

CAKE.

One pound of flour, one of butter, one of sugar, ten eggs, one pound of raisins, one pound of English walnuts, one-half pound of figs, one-half pound of citron, one large teaspoon of mace, one tablespoon of molasses with a speck of soda, one tablespoon of brandy or wine. Beat the eggs separately.

IMPERIAL CAKE.

Ten eggs, one pound of butter, one pound of sugar, one of flour, one of English walnuts, one of raisins, one-quarter of a pound of citron, one tablespoon of mace, one wine glass of brandy.

NUT CAKE.

One cup sugar, one-half cup of butter, one-half cup of milk, two cups of flour, two eggs, one teaspoon Royal Baking Powder, one cup of nuts and one cup of raisins chopped together.

PLYMOUTH CAKE.

One-half cup of butter, one and one-half cups of sugar, two cups of flour, three eggs, two-thirds of a cup of milk, one teaspoon of Royal Baking Powder.

PORK CAKE.

One-half pound of pork chopped fine, pour over this one cup of boiling water, then add one cup of sugar, one-half cup of molasses, one teaspoonful of soda, two pounds of fruit more or less, four and one-half cups of flour according to the fruit used, spices of all kinds, and lemon.

Use Old Reliable Tomatoes.

MARBLE CAKE.

Light: Whites of four eggs beaten to a froth, one and one-half cups of white sugar, one-half cup of butter beaten with the sugar, one-half cup of sweet milk with one-half teaspoon of soda, one teaspoon of cream tartar in two and one-half cups of flour. Flavor with lemon.

Dark: Yolks of four eggs, one whole one, one-half cup of butter, one cup of sugar, one-half cup of molasses with one-half teaspoon of soda, two cups of flour, spice of all kinds, and fruit. Add a little more flour for the fruit.

BRIDE'S CAKE.

Two coffee cups of sugar, whites of nine eggs, small cup of butter. Cream the butter and sugar. Beat the whites to a stiff froth and add one cup of milk with a small cup of corn starch dissolved in it, one even teaspoon of cream tartar, one-half teaspoon of soda dissolved in a little water, two cups of flour. Sift the cream tartar in the flour. Mix well the butter, sugar and eggs; add the corn starch and milk but do not beat, then add the flour. Mix again. Add the soda the last thing and put in the oven instantly. Have a slow, steady fire. Flavor with almond.

WALNUT CAKE.

Whites of five eggs, one and one-half cups of sugar, one-half cup of butter, one-half cup of milk, two cups of flour, one-half teaspoon soda, one of cream tartar. Cream butter and sugar with the hand, add one cup of flour, with cream tartar, soda in milk, last cup flour. Beat up light, add vanilla and one large cup of walnuts.

DELICATE CAKE.

One cup of sugar, one-half cup of butter, whites of four eggs, two cups of flour, one teaspoon Royal Baking Powder, one cup of milk, one teaspoonful almond.

WHITE MOUNTAIN CAKE.

Six eggs, six cups of flour, three cups of sugar, two cups of butter, one cup of milk, one-half teaspoonful of soda, one teaspoonful of cream tartar.

Use Old Reliable Corn

ICE CREAM CAKE.

Two cups of sugar, one cup of butter, one cup of milk, three scant cups of flour, one teaspoonful of cream tartar, one-half of soda, flavor with vanilla, white of three eggs put in last, yolks not used. This makes two thin loaves to put filling between.

Filling: Two tablespoons of gelatine dissolved in six teaspoons of cold water; pour this over one cup and a half of powdered sugar, beat half an hour. Flavor with vanilla. Butter tin in which cake is to bake, in this spread the filling and let it stand over night. Put this between the cakes with white of an egg.

DARK CAKE.

One-half coffee cup of sugar, one-half coffee cup of molasses, one-half cup of buttermilk, one-half cup of butter, one-half cup of raisins, one egg, one teaspoonsful of soda, one half teaspoonful of all kinds of spice.

GOLD CAKE.

One cup of sugar, one-half cup of butter, the yolks of three eggs, one-half cup of milk, one teaspoonful of cream tartar, one-half teaspoonful of soda, two scant cups of flour. After adding the flour, beat well and then stir in lightly the white of one egg beaten very stiff.

LUNCH CAKE.

Two cups of sugar, one cup of butter, three eggs, one cup of milk, two teaspoonfuls Royal Baking Powder, flour enough for a stiff batter. Roll out about half an inch thick and sprinkle with cinnamon; roll up lightly, cut off slices half an inch thick and roll them in sugar. Bake quickly.

HATTIE CAKE.

Four eggs, two cups of sugar, one large spoonful of butter, one cup of sweet milk, three cups of flour, two teaspoonfuls of Royal Baking Powder; flavor. Bake in layers.

STRAWBERRY SHORTCAKE.

One quart of flour, three tablespoons of butter, one large cup of sour cream, one egg, one tablespoonful of white sugar, one teaspoonful of soda.

Use Mansfield's Flavoring Extracts

ORANGE CAKE NO. 1.

The yolks of four eggs beaten with one and one-half cups of sugar. Add the whites of two eggs beaten stiff, one-half of ice water with one-half teaspoon of soda in it, two cups of flour with a teaspoon of cream tartar, juice and grated rind of one orange. Bake in square pans, and frost between the layers.

Frosting: Two cups of sugar and two-thirds of a cup of water boiled without stiring till it will thread on the point of a skewer; pour it in a fine stream over the beaten whites of two eggs to which a saltspoon of cream tartar has been added, beating steadily all the time. Add slowly the juice and grated rind of one orange and beat till it will harden on the cake.

ORANGE CAKE NO. 2.

One-half cup of butter and one cup of sugar beaten to a cream, whites of four eggs, one and one-half cups of flour, one-half cup of milk, one teaspoonful of cream tartar, one-half teaspoonful of soda, one tablespoonful of orange juice and a little of grated rind.

Frosting: One cup of sugar, one-third of a cup of hot water boiled until it will string. Have ready the white of one egg beaten stiff, add one saltspoonful of cream tartar; pour the syrup slowly on the egg, beating all the time, add one teaspoonful of orange juice and a little of the grated rind; beat until it will go on the cake without running.

SPICE CAKE.

One and one-half cups of sugar, one-half cup of molasses, one cup of butter, one cup of milk, three cups of flour, two eggs, one-half teaspoon of soda, salt, and spice of all kinds.

SNOW CAKE.

One cup of butter, one cup of sweet milk, two cups of sugar, three cups of flour, whites of five eggs, two teaspoons of Royal Baking Powder, a little mace.

SOUR CREAM FILLING.

One cup of sour cream beaten, one cup of raisins stoned and chopped, one-half cup of chopped figs.

Our Teas take the lead every time

ONE-EGG CAKE.

One cup of sugar, one-half cup of butter one egg, one-half cup of milk, one teaspoonful of Royal Baking Powder. one cup of currants, two cups of flour.

COFFEE CAKES.

One quart of flour, two teaspoons of Royal Baking Powder. piece of butter size of egg rubbed into the flour. Measure one of sugar, putting two-thirds of it into the flour; mix with milk or milk and water; roll out until one-half inch in thickness. Spread the remainder of the sugar and cinnamon on and roll up like jelly cake, cutting off in pieces one-half inch in thickness. One egg is an improvement, but it can be made without.

COFFEE CAKE.

Two cups of brown sugar, one cup of molasses, one cup of butter, one cup of strong coffee, four cups of flour, four eggs, one teaspoonful of soda, two teaspoonfuls each of cassia, cloves, allspice and nutmeg, one pound each of raisins and currants, one-quarter of citron.

CREAM CAKE.

Two eggs. one-half cup of sugar, one teaspoon of cream tartar, one-half teaspoon of soda, a pinch of salt, one cup of flour.

Filling: One cup of milk (boiling), two or three tablespoons of sugar, one egg, one tablespoon of flour add to the milk. After cooling, flavor to taste.

Frosting made of the whites of two eggs, four tablespoons pulverized sugar; spread on cake and cover with cocoanut.

BEAUTIFUL CAKE.

One and one-half cups of sugar, one cup of butter, three eggs, two and one-half cups of cups of flour, one-half teaspoon of soda, one of cream tartar, one-half cup milk. A good cake to keep.

COLD WATER CAKE.

Two eggs, one cup of sugar, one-half cup of butter, one teaspoon of cream tartar, one-half teaspoon of soda, one and a half cups flour, one-half cup cold water, lemon or vanilla.

Mansfield's Coffees are far famed

MOTHER HUBBARD CAKE.

One cup of eggs, one and one-half cups of sugar, one cup of butter, one and one-half cups of flour, one-half teaspoon Royal Baking Powder. Beat flour and butter to a cream; beat eggs and sugar very light, put all together, add baking powder last.

WHITE CUP CAKE.

One cup of butter, two of sugar, three of flour, one of sweet milk, one teaspoonful Royal Baking Powder, the whites of four eggs well beaten.

SPONGE CAKE NO. 1.

Beat well together the yolks of ten eggs with one pound of powered sugar, then stir in the whites beaten to a stiff froth. Beat the whole together ten or fifteen minutes, then stir in gradually one-half pound sifted flour. Flavor with nutmeg or the grated rind of half a lemon. Bake immediately.

SPONGE CAKE NO. 2.

Three eggs, one and a half cups of sugar, one-half cup of cold water, two cups of flour, one teaspoonful Royal Baking Powder, pinch of salt, flavor with vanilla or lemon.

MOONY CAKE.

Six eggs, two coffee cups of sugar, one coffee cup of butter, one coffee cup of milk, two teaspoonfuls Royal Baking Powder, three coffee cups of flour.

DAYTON CAKE.

One cup of butter, two cups of sugar, three cups of flour, one-half cup of milk one-half teaspoonful of soda, one teaspoonful of cream tartar, six eggs. This is very nice and will keep three months, spiced a good deal with two pounds of raisins, two pounds of currants, one pound of citron chopped.

DEXTER CAKE.

Rub a half cup of butter and one cup of sugar to a cream, add the whites of three eggs well beaten; then add a half cup of milk in which is dissolved half teaspoonful of soda, beat well then add two cups of flour in which is stirred

Specialty of Imported Canned Goods

one teaspoonful of cream tartar; one teaspoonful of vanilla. Bake in three tins.

Frosting: Yolk of three eggs, one cup of pulverized sugar, beat fifteen minutes; flavor and spread between the layers and on top.

CIRCLE CAKE.

One cup of sugar, one-half cup of butter, two eggs, one-half cup of milk, one-half teaspoon of soda, one teaspoon of cream tartar, two cups of flour.

Frosting for same: One cup of sugar, one-half cup of milk, one square of chocolate, a bit of butter.

CHOCOLATE PIE.

Two cups of sugar, two-thirds of a cup of butter, yolks of five eggs, whites of two, one cup of milk, three and one-half cups of flour, one teaspoon Royal Baking Powder.

Mixture for filling: Whites of three eggs, one cup and a half of sugar, three tablespoonfuls of grated chocolate, one teaspoonful of vanilla.

Bake the cake on Washington pie plates and spread the mixture between the layers and over the top of each pie, first allowing the pie to cool. This makes two pies.

POUND CAKE.

One pound of sugar, one pound of flour, three-quarters of a pound of butter, two tablespoonfuls of brandy, one-quarter teaspoonful of soda, eight eggs, one-quarter pound of citron, one pound of raisins.

CORNUCOPIAS.

One and one-half cups of sugar, two cups of flour, one-half cup of cold water, three eggs, one teaspoonful of cream tartar, one-half teaspoonful of soda, little salt. Bake in small tins and roll up like cornucopias.

BLUEBERRY CAKE.

Four cups of flour, one cup of sugar, two eggs, one-half cup of melted butter, one and one-half teaspoons of cream tartar, one teaspoon of soda, one pint of berries rubbed in a dish of flour.

Try Millar's Royal Paragon Cheese

TEA CAKE.

Three cups of flour, one teaspoon of cream tartar, a little salt, butter size of an egg, half cup of sugar. Mix together, then add one and one-half cups of milk, one egg, and half teaspoon of soda.

POVERTY CAKE.

One cup of butter, one and one-half cups of sugar, three cups of flour, one and one-half cups of raisins (stoned), one cup of milk, two eggs, one half teaspoon of soda in one-half cup of molases, one-half teaspoon of cinnamon, clove and nutmeg.

CUP CAKE.

Two cups sugar, one cup of milk, four eggs, one-half cup of butter, two teaspoonfuls of Royal Baking Powder, three and one-half cups of flour.

LEOPARD CAKE.

One and one-quarter pounds of butter, one and one-quarter pounds of sugar, one and one-quarter pounds of flour, a tablespoon of mace. Divide the quantity for dark part. Three pounds of raisins, one-half pound of citron, one scant cup of molases, one-quarter of a teaspoon of soda lemon and brandy, one teaspoon of clove and cinnamon. Drop in like marble cake.

CHOCOLATE CAKE.

One cup of sugar, one-half cup of butter, one-half cup of milk, one cup of flour, one-half cup of cornstarch, whites of three eggs, one teaspoon of Royal Baking Powder, two squares of chocolate (melted).

LEMON CAKE

Two cups of sugar, one-half cup of butter, one cup of milk, three and one half cups of flour, three eggs, two teaspoonfuls of cream tartar, one teaspoonful of soda. Bake in four layers.

Filling: Grate the rind of three small or two large lemons and add the juice with one cup of sugar, one egg, one-half cup of water, one teaspoonful of flour, and one teaspoonful of butter. Boil until it thickens, then place between the layers of the cake.

Evaporated Fruits in their season

CORNSTARCH CAKE.

One and one-half cups of sugar, one-half cup of butter, one-half cup of milk, one-half cup of cornstarch, one and one-half cups of flour, one teaspoonful of Royal Baking Powder, whites of six eggs beaten to a froth and stirred in last.

MOLLIE'S CAKE.

Two cups of sugar, one-half cup of butter, three cups of flour, one cup of milk, four eggs, yolks and whites beaten separately, two teaspoonfuls of Royal Baking Powder. Sift cream tartar and soda with the flour, cream butter and sugar, add beaten yolks of eggs, mix well, then the flour and milk, and lastly whites of eggs.

FARMER'S FRUIT CAKE.

Wash thoroughly three cups of dried apples, and soak over night. Drain off the water through a seive, chop them slightly, then simmer two hours in three cup of molasses, then add two eggs, one cup of sugar, one cup of sweet milk or water, three quarters of a cup of butter, one-half teaspoonful of soda, flour to make quite a stiff batter, cinnamon, clove and other spices to suit the taste.

HARLEQUIN CAKE.

One cup of butter, two cups of sugar, three eggs (yolks), one cup of milk, three cups of flour, one measure each of Horsford's bread preparation, one teaspoonful of cream tartar, one-half teaspoon of soda, three eggs, (whites), mix in the order given. Then divide the dough in four equal parts: have two parts the color of the dough, flavor one with extract of orange, the other with vanilla, color the third with two squares of chocolate melted, color the fourth with pink coloring and flavor with strawberry, then bake each. When done lay a light, then a chocolate, then a light, then pink. Between the layers spread lemon jelly, and frost with white frosting.

Lemon jelly: Beat one egg, add one cup of water, the grated rind and juice of one lemon, pour this slowly over one cup of sugar mixed with two tablespoonfuls of flour. Cook until quite smooth.

Best Results from Mansfield's Extracts

ANGEL CAKE.

One cup of flour, one and one-half cups of sugar, one teaspoonful of cream tartar. Sift the whole four times. Beat the whites of eleven eggs to a froth on a large platter, add one teaspoonful of vanilla, then add the flour, sugar, and a little salt very lightly. Bake in an ungreased pan slowly forty minutes, the pan must have a tube in it; let it remain in the pan until cold.

TAVE'S CAKE.

Yolks of six eggs, one whole egg, one and a half cups of sugar, one-half cup of milk, one-half cup of butter, one-half cup of cornstarch, one and one-half cups of flour, one-half teaspoonful soda, one teaspoonful cream tartar.

WHIPPED CREAM CAKE.

Three eggs, one cup of sugar, one-half cup of sweet milk, one teaspoonful cream tartar, one-half of soda (in the milk), one cup of flour; vanilla. Bake in layers.

Filling: Whip one large cup of sweet cream, three tablespoonfuls of sugar, and flavor with vanilla.

SPICE CAKE.

One cup of molsses, with one teaspoonful of soda, one cup of sugar, one cup of butter, one cup of sour milk, two eggs, one cup of raisins, one teaspoon of all kinds of spices, flour not to stiff, beat thoroughly.

MELTED BUTTER CAKE.

One and one-half cups of sugar, two-thirds of a cup of milk, three eggs, one teaspoon of cream tartar, one-half teaspoon of soda. Add one-half cup of melted butter the last thing before putting into the oven.

TEA CAKES.

One scant half cup of sugar, two eggs one-half cup of melted butter, one and one fourth cups of milk, one teaspoon of soda, two teaspoons of cream tartar, flour to make a stiff batter. Bake in gem pans.

DELICIOUS CAKE.

Two cups of sugar, one cup of butter, one cup of milk,

Latest Specialties in Grocery line at Mansfield's

three eggs, one teaspoonful Royal Baking Powder, three cups of flour.

CREAM CAKES.

One cup of boiling water, one-half cup of butter, one cup of flour, and three eggs. Let the water and butter come to a boil, then stir in the flour and let it cook a minute or two. Take from the stove and break in the eggs, one at a time. Stir till thoroughly mixed, then drop in pans. This will make a dozen cake . Bake in quite a hot oven until the butter, which comes to the surface in bubbles, disappears. Cool in the pans.

Filling : One cup of sugar, one-half cup of flour, one egg, one pint of milk. Cook like custard. Flavor with vanilla.

NELL'S CHOCOLATE CAKE NO. 1.

One cup of sugar, one-half cup of butter, one-half cup of milk, two eggs, two cups of flour (two-thirds full), one even teaspoon soda.

Mixture : One-half cake chocolate, grated, one-half cup of milk, two heaping tablespoon of sugar, yolk of one egg. Cook until it thickens, stirring all the time, and mix with the cake. Flavor with vanilla.

CHOCOLATE CAKE NO. 2.

One cup sugar, one-half cup of butter, one-half cup of water, one and one-half cups of flour, two eggs, one square of chocolate, one teaspoonful cream tartar, one-half teaspoon of soda, one teaspoon vanilla. Beat butter and sugar to a cream ; dissolve soda in water ; mix cream tartar in flour ; dissolve chocolate and beat in before putting in the flour. Bake in one sheet.

CHOCOLATE CAKE NO. 3.

One cup of sugar, two eggs, one-half cup of milk or water, two cups of flour, one-half cup of butter, one teaspoon Royal Baking Powder, one square of chocolate ; vanilla.

LIGHT CAKE.

One cup of butter, two cups of sugar, two cups of flour, one cup of milk, one cup of cornstarch, whites of five eggs,

Edam, Pineapple, Cream and Domestic Cheese

one teaspoonful of soda, two teaspoonfuls of cream tartar. Flavor with vanilla. This is enough for two cakes, and the cakes should be cold before the frosting is put on. Bake the cake in sheets.

Caramel frosting: Two cups of sugar, one cup of milk, piece of butter size of walnut. Boil twenty minutes and then take from the stove and beat rapidly until cool enough to spread on the cake. Melt some chocolate and put a thin coating over the top of the boiled frosting.

LEMON CAKE.

Make this cake the same as "Light Cake," omitting the flavoring. If preferred, take an extra cup of flour instead of the cornstarch. Bake in thin sheets.

Lemon filling: Juice and grated rind of one lemon; one egg, one cup of sugar, one teaspoonful of flour, butter size of a walnut. Stir it over the steam of a teakettle until thoroughly heated. The boiled frosting is very nice on this cake.

SILVER CAKE.

One cup of butter, two cups of sugar, three cups of flour, one-half cup of milk, one teaspoonful of cream tartar and one-half of soda, whites of eight eggs.

TEA KISSES.

Half a cup of butter, two cups of flour, one cup of sugar, two eggs beaten stiff, two tablespoons of milk, two teaspoons Royal Baking Powder. Dip out by the teaspoonful; spreas far apart on a pan. Sprinkle with powdered sugar and bake in a quick oven. It takes but a few minutes, and they are very nice.

BROWN SUGAR CAKE.

Two and one-half cups of brown sugar, one cup of butter, one half cup of milk, three eggs, three cups of flour, two teaspoonfuls of Royal Baking Powder, one-third of a teaspoonful of nutmeg, one teaspoonful of molasses, one cup of currants, one cup of raisins, one-quarter of a pound of citron.

JAMES CAKE.

One and one-half cups of sugar, one cup of butter, two eggs, two teaspoonfuls of molasses, one-half cup sour milk,

Day and Martin's Blacking

one large teaspoonful of soda, two and one-half cups of flour, all kind of spice.

GOOD ONE EGG CAKE.

One-half cup of butter, one and one-half cups of sugar, one cup of sweet milk, one egg, two teaspoonfuls Royal Baking Powder, one cup of raisins chopped fine, three very scant cups of sifted flour, flavor.

FILLING AND FROSTING FOR CAKE

RAISIN FILLING

Take one cup of white sugar, put it into a tin basin with enough water to dissolve it; let it boil until it will harden in cold water. Have ready a cupful of stoned and chopped raisins, then beat the white of one egg to a stiff froth, put with the raisins into the boiling sugar. Stir briskly, and while warm put it between the layers of the cake.

CHOCOLATE FROSTING.

One cup of sugar, one-half cup of milk, piece of butter half the size of an egg, one square of chocolate; boil until brittle. Beat it a while before putting on the cake.

FIG FILLING.

One cup of sugar, a scant half cup of water, boil till it forms a thick syrup and add half a pound of figs chopped fine. Cook two or three minutes, take from fire and add the juice of one lemon and the whites of two eggs beaten stiff. When taken from the stove it should be too thick to run.

FROSTING.

One cup of sugar, four tablespoonfuls of water, boil without stirring until it ropes; white of one egg well beaten, one-quarter of a teaspoonful of cream tartar, flavor. Pour the boiling syrup on the egg, slowly beating all the time. Beat until cool enough to spread.

For Chocolate Frosting add two tablespoonfuls or more of grated chocolate to the egg before pouring on the syrup.

Red and Blue Sugar for Cake

COFFEE ICING.

One-half gill of strong coffee in a sauce-pan, add one cupful of confectioners' sugar. Stir over the fire until warm. Spread on cake.

PINK COLORING FOR CAKE AND CREAMS.

One-quarter ounce each of cochineal, alum, cream of tartar and salt of tartars, one gill of boiling water, one-quarter pound of sugar. To the first three ingredients add the boiling water and put in a porcelain stew-pan. Let it stand on the stove, without boiling, for twenty-five minutes; add the salts of tartar very gradually, stirring all the time; add the sugar, strain and bottle it. Use one or two teaspoonfuls, according to the shade desired.

FROSTING WITHOUT EGGS.

Put four tablespoonfuls of sweet milk in a dish over a slow fire; when it simmers stir in slowly one cup of granulated sugar, let it boil five minutes without stirring, then set the dish in cold water or on ice and stir to a cream. This frosting does not flake off, and with a little practice is perfect. Flavor according to taste. If it gets hard too soon heat again.

BANANA FILLING FOR CAKE.

One cup of fine sugar, one half cup of boiling water, boil until quite thick; white of one egg, beaten stiff. Pour boiling mixture over the egg, stirring constantly; add three bananas sliced thin, beat the whole together until cool and thick enough to spread without running.

COCOANUT FILLING.

One grated cocoanut; to one-half of this add whites of three eggs, beaten stiff, one cup of powdered sugar; lay this between the cake. Mix with the remaining half of cocoanut four tablespoons of powdered sugar; spread on top for frosting

Confectioners' and Powdered Sugar

ELASTIC ✸ STARCH

A great invention. Requires no cooking. Makes collars and cuffs stiff and nice, as when first bought new.

This Starch is made entirely different from all other Starches, and is the only starch in the United States that is put up by men who have a practical experience in the laundry business. How to laundry linen has been kept a secret long enough, that can and should be done in every family. By using this Starch your Shirts, Cuffs and Collars, will be just as stiff and nice as when first bought new. A few other advantages this Starch possesses over all other Starch is: It requires no cooking, keeps the iron from sticking and linen from blistering while ironing. The manufacturers offer one hundred dollars in gold, if this Starch proves injurious to the finest of linen.

J. C. Hubinger Bros' Co., are the inventors and originators of the ELASTIC STARCH. They didn't have to borrow and steal the name and fame of their neighbors in order to sell this Starch. Beware of worthless imitations which have recently been put into the market to deceive the public. Be sure that the name ELECTRIC, cut of the flat-iron, and name of J. C. Hubinger Bros' Co., New Haven, Conn., is upon the package without which it can not be genuine. Always in stock at

W. H. Mansfield & Co's., Putnam.

FOR BEST RESULTS USE

Mansfield's Flavoring Extracts
— Perfectly Pure, Extra Strong —

FULL WEIGHT.

Endorsed by the best trade in this section.

None better and few if any Equal.

Don't Spoil Your Food
—BY USING—

POOR EXTRACTS

W. H. Mansfield & Co., Proprietors.

MANSFIELD'S GROUND SPICES

ARE ABSOLUTELY PURE.

Ground from Selected and Best Spices by experienced spice millers, expressly for us, and not one single particle of adulteration ever had, or will ever be added to them.

Of course they cost more than ordinary, and so called pure spices, but they are certainly worth more, as they are stronger; thus in reality costing less.

For Sale in boxes and bulk.

W. H. Mansfield & Co. Prop.

Canned ✳ Goods

Largest Variety, Largest Stock, Finest Quality, Freshest Goods most carefully Packed in Connecticut will be found at

W. H. MANSFIELD & CO'S

Consisting of all kinds Fruits, Vegetables, Meats, Fish, Soups, Potted Meats and Poultry. French Vegetables in glass and tin. California Fruits in glass.

OLD RELIABLE CORN

———AND———

OLD RELIABLE TOMATOES

Packed expressly for us from selected stock. The Corn is extremely TENDER, SWEET and free from silk.

The Tomatoes are also packed with extreme care from Perfection variety; being ripe, yet always perfectly sound.

As we are heavy buyers in all lines of Canned Goods, we are enabled to give lowest prices.

W. H. Mansfield & Co., Putnam.

Cookies and Gingerbread.

MOLASSES DROPS.

One and one-half cups of molasses, one-half cup of butter, one-half cup of milk, one egg, one and one-half teaspoons of soda, three and one-half cups of flour.

GINGER SNAPS.

One cup of molasses, one cup of light brown sugar, one-half cup of butter and lard, one teaspoonful of salt, one teaspoonful of ginger, three scant teaspoonfuls of cream tartar, one-half cup of boiling water in which stir two teaspoonfuls of soda. Pour over the other ingredients and add flour. Roll thin.

SUGAR COOKIES No. 1.

One and one-half cups of sugar, one cup of melted butter, one cup of sour milk, one egg, one teaspoonful of soda. Beat egg, stir in the other ingredients with just flour enough so that the paste can be handled and moulded. Roll thin and bake light but quickly.

SUGAR COOKIES No. 2.

One cup of sugar, one cup of butter, one egg, three tablespoons of buttermilk, one-half teaspoon of soda; mix quite hard.

SUGAR COOKIES No. 3.

Two cups of sugar and one cup of butter beaten to cream; yolks of three eggs beaten and added, one teaspoon of soda, two tablespoons of sour milk; flour to make stiff. Roll thin.

MOLASSES COOKIES No. 1.

One and one-half cups of molasses boiled ten minutes, one-half cup of butter, one teaspoon of soda, flour to make stiff. Roll thin and bake quickly.

Imported Vegetables in Glass.

MOLASSES COOKIES No. 2.

One cup of sugar, two cups of molasses, three-fourths of a cup of butter, two-thirds of a cup of boiling water, two small teaspoons of soda dissolved in the hot water, one teaspoon ginger; salt. Knead as little as possible. Roll thin and bake quickly.

BELKNAP COOKIES.

One cup of sugar, one cup of butter, three eggs, one quart of flour, one and one-half teaspoons of Royal baking powder, one-half nutmeg.

BAKER'S SQUARES.

Two cups of molasses, one heaping cup of butter, one cup of sugar, two-thirds of a cup of sour milk, two tablespoonsful of ginger, two teaspoonfuls of soda in the molasses and one in the milk, two eggs, flour to knead. Mix over night. Roll thick and cut with a square cutter. Bake a light brown.

GINGER COOKIES.

One cup of sugar, one cup of molasses, one cup of butter, three teaspoons of ginger, one egg, two teaspoons of soda dissolved in six tablespoons of hot water, salt to taste. Bake in a quick oven.

SPONGE GINGERBREAD.

One and one-half cups of molasses, one-half cup of melted butter, one good teaspoonful each of soda, salt and ginger, one cup of boiling water, flour enough for a thin batter as for sponge cake. Bake in thin sheets in a quick oven.

SNICKER-NOODLES.

Two eggs, two cups of sugar, three-quarters of a cup of butter, one cup of milk, two teaspoons Royal Baking Powder, four cups of flour. Drop in buttered pans. Sift over cinnamon and sugar just before putting into the oven.

HERMITS.

One and one-half cups of sugar, one cup of butter, three eggs, one-half teaspoonful of soda, one teaspoonful each of nutmeg, cassia and allspice, one cup raisins chopped fine, one-half cup of citron, chopped, flour to roll. Quick oven.

Mansfield's Spices are Perfection.

CHOCOLATE COOKIES.

One cup of butter, one and one half cups of sugar, two eggs, one teaspoon of soda dissolved in a little milk, four cups flour, two teaspoons cream tartar, two squares melted chocolate

MARIE'S NUT WAFERS.

Two eggs, one and three-quarters cups sugar, one-half cup butter, one quart nuts chopped fine, as little flour as possible to roll thin.

SOFT GINGERBREAD.

One-half cup of molasses, one-half cup of sugar, one egg, butter size of an egg, one-half cup of buttermilk, one teaspoon of soda, one cup of raisins, chopped, two cups of flour.

COFFEE GINGERBREAD

One egg, one cup of molasses, one cup of coffee, one teaspoonful of soda, one-half cup of butter, one-quarter of a teaspoonful of all kinds of spice, one-half cup of sugar, three cups of flour. Bake in a thin sheet.

NICE DOUGHNUTS No. 1.

Two eggs, one cup of sugar, one tablespoonful of lard, one cup of buttermilk or sour milk, a teaspoonful of soda, a little salt and nutmeg.

DOUGHNUTS No. 2.

One cup of sugar, two eggs, two-thirds of a cup of sweet milk, two teaspoons of Royal Baking Powder, two and one-half teaspoons of melted butter, nutmeg, salt, and a tiny bit of cinnamon. Mix soft.

TRIFLES.

Beat one egg to a stiff froth, add a little salt and flour enough to make very stiff. Roll as thin as a wafer and fry in hot lard.

BAKER'S GINGERBREAD.

One cup of molasses, one cup of sugar, two eggs, one cup of sour milk, one cup of butter, three teaspoonfuls of soda, one teaspoonful of ginger; flour enough to roll; cut in quite thick squares: just before putting into the oven cover with the beaten white of one egg.

Old Reliable Soap makes the clothes white.

WARM GINGERBREAD.

One cup of molasses, one cup of sugar, four tablespoonfuls of butter, two teaspoonfuls each of soda and ginger, two cups of flour; salt, one cup of boiling water put in just before putting into the oven.

COFFEE CAKES (GERMAN).

One quart of flour, one-half cup of butter, one cup of sugar, one cup of sweet milk, two teaspoons of cream tartar, one teaspoon of soda. Mix and roll an inch thick. Sprinkle on the dough one-third of a cup of sugar mixed with one teaspoon of cinnamon, and roll like a jelly roll. Cut off the thickness of cookies and bake, being careful not to have them too near together in the pan. These are very nice to eat with coffee in place of doughnuts.

COTTAGE CHEESE.

Heat sour milk with a gentle heat (it is a good way to set the pan over a kettle of warm but not boiling water) until the whey separates from the curd. Pour off the whey with care, put the curd into a bag, and hang it to drip for several hours. Do not squeeze it. Work it with a spoon or with the hands until it is soft and even, salt it, add a little cream or butter, mould into round balls, or leave it to be served in small saucers. It should be eaten while fresh.

BONNY-CLABBER, OR LOPPERED MILK.

Set a china or glass dish of skimmed milk away in a warm place, covered. When it turns—i. e., becomes a smooth, firm, but not tough cake, like blancmange—serve in the same dish. Cut out carefully with a large spoon, and put in saucers with cream, powdered sugar, and nutmeg to taste. It is better if set on the ice for an hour before it is brought to the table. Do not let it stand until the whey separates from the curd. Few people know how delicious this healthful and simple dessert can be made, if eaten before it becomes tough and tart, with a liberal allowance of cream and sugar. There are not many jellies and creams superior to it.

Try Our Superior Ground Ginger

BENSDORP'S
Royal Dutch
Cocoas and Chocolates

See that the cover of every can of Cocoa bears this stamp.

For all choice **Cooking** purposes, as well as **Drinking,** this Cocoa is not only the **best,** but more convenient and economical than chocolate in cake form. Try it once in place of what you are now using. For sale and recommended by

W. H. MANSFIELD & CO.

PIES.

PASTRY FOR ONE PIE.

One cup of flour, one large spoonful of butter and lard mixed, one-half teaspoon of salt. Rub the lard into the flour and wet with ice water until it is a soft dough ; roll into a thin sheet and spread butter over it. Fold the corners over it and roll.

PUFF PASTE.

One half pound of flour. Make a hole in the middle and put in a pinch of salt, then mix with the hand with cold water. About one gill is necessary. Then roll to one-quar- of an inch thick ; spread over it one-half pound of butter as evenly as possible, fold it in four ; roll it again, fold as before four times, for extra, five times. Use only flour sufficient to keep it from sticking. Cut it with a paste cutter and color with the yolk of an egg and a little water. A quick oven as for roasting beef. Do not open the oven for ten minutes. They will be done in fifteen minutes.

TART PASTE.

Half cup of butter, half cup of lard, mixed, two cups of flour, a half cup of sweet milk, one teaspoonful of cream tar- tar and a half teaspoonful of soda.

LEMON CUSTARD PIE.

One cup of scalded milk, one-half cup sugar, two table- spoons of flour, three eggs Take out whites of two eggs for frosting. Grated rind of one lemon, piece of butter size of an egg. Beat together, then put in hot milk. When slightly cool add lemon juice. Bake crust first, then spread on filling and frost. Brown in oven. Beat frosting on a plate a long time after the sugar is added.

We always sell Pure Lard

LEMON PIE.

Two large lemons, one cup of water, one cup of sugar, four eggs, two tablespoons of cornstarch or three of flour. Grate the rind of one lemon, squeeze out juice and pulp of both, add sugar and water; separate white from yolks, beat yolks and add to lemon; stir well and put in steamer, let it steam until hot. This makes two pies. While steaming line two plates with paste and bake, making holes in crust so it will not blister. By the time crust is made filling is hot enough to stir in, starch having been mixed with half a cup of water, let it steam until thick. Beat whites of eggs to a stiff froth, add four tablespoons of sugar and half a teaspoon of lemon extract. Frost with this.

LEMON PIE (WITH FROSTING.)

Allow the grated rind and juice of two lemons, two cups of sugar, three eggs, and a piece of butter as large as an egg. Rub smooth in some cold water two tablespoonfuls of cornstarch. Have ready two cups of boiling water in a saucepan, and stir into it the cornstarch until it looks clear. Then pour into a dish and add the sugar and butter. When it becomes nearly cool, add the yolks of three eggs and one of the whites, beaten together, the grated rind and juice of the lemons, and bake in two deep plates of medium size, lined with a delicate crust. Beat up the whites with two spoonfuls of sugar, very stiff, spread this over the pies after they are baked, sprinkle with sugar and brown a few minutes in the oven.

MOCK MINCE PIE.

Six soda crackers, two cups of cold water, one cup of molasses one cup of brown sugar, one and one-half cups of melted butter, one cup of chopped raisins, one cup of currants two eggs beaten light, one tablespoonful of cinnamon, one teaspoonful of nutmeg, one of clove, one of salt and one of black pepper. Wineglass of brandy or cider. This is enough for four large pies.

BOILED CIDER PIE.

One quart of cider boiled down to one cupful, one heap-

Largest line of Crackers in the County

ing cup sugar, two eggs, one heaping tablespoon of flour. Before pouring on the crust add four teaspoons cold water and one teaspoon vanilla. Bake with two crusts.

SQUASH PIE.

One cup of strained squash, one egg, one and one-quarter cups of milk, one-half cup of sugar, nutmeg. and salt. Enough for one pie.

CREAM PIE.

Line a deep pie plate with a rich paste; beat the white of an egg, add one pint of cream, sugar to taste; beat all together well but not whip; flavor with nutmeg or vanilla and bake as a custard pie.

APPLE PIE NO. 1.

Pare and slice enough apples to fill the plate or plates; add one cup of sugar to a plate. a little butter. two tablespoons of water, and flavor with nutmeg, cinnamon, or extract of lemon. Bake until the apples are soft.

APPLE PIE NO, 2.

Stew enough apples for four pies, four eggs, two-thirds of a cup of butter, one cup of sugar, a tablespoon of extract of lemon.

BRAMBLES.

One coffee cup of raisins chopped fine with one lemon. Add two crackers rolled fine, one cup of sugar, one egg, one-fourth cup of milk; mix thoroughly. Have pastry cut into squares and place a tablespoonful of the mixture in each one. Moisten the edges with milk to prvent running out, and fold over. This will make eighteen.

BANBERRIES.

One pound of raisins seeded and chopped, the juice and grated rind of two lemons, two cups of sugar, two eggs. Make a rich crust, cut out with saucer, put a teaspoonful on each, double up like a turnover, brush over with milk and bake. This makes forty.

PUMPKIN PIE.

Pare and take out the seeds of a small pumpkin, stew it

Finest line of Canned Goods in this section

dry and strain through a colander; add two quarts of milk, three eggs, three tablespoons molasses, and some sugar. Season with cinnamon, ginger and salt.

LEMON PATTIES

Line small pattie pans with puff paste and fill with the following mixture: Three eggs, two cups of sugar, grated rind and juice of two lemons. Bake lightly.

RHUBARB PIE.

One cup of sugar, one egg, a small piece of butter, one lemon, juice and rind, two tablespoons of flour or cornstarch, one cup of chopped rhubarb, a little salt. Bake with two crusts.

MINCE MEAT NO. 1.

Five pounds of meat, two pounds of suet, two pounds of chopped raisins, one pound of whole raisins, one peck of apples, two bowls of molasses, one bowl of vinegar, four bowls of cider, four bowls of sugar, three tablespoonfuls of cloves, three of cassia, three of allspice, and two of salt. Three nutmegs, citron, currants and jelly if you like.

MINCE MEAT NO. 2.

Three and one-half pounds of beef, two of suet, seven of apples, three and one-half of raisins, stoned, one of citron and one of currants, one-half ounce of mace, one of clove, one of allspice, one of cinnamon, and one-half of nutmeg, one quart of cider, one pint of molasses, two pounds sugar, one-half cup of salt. Sometimes a little change from the this according to taste.

MINCE PIE MEAT NO. 3.

Two pounds of beef, four of apples, three of raisins, two of sugar; one teaspoonful of clove and one of cinnamon, one-half pound of citron, one quart of cider, three pints of cranberries chopped fine, one pint of molasses, a little butter when the pies are made.

Headquarters for Dried Fruits

HOT PUDDINGS

BLUEBERRY PUDDING.

Two cups of sweet milk, one cup of sugar, two eggs well beaten, one tablespoonful of butter, four cups of flour, with one teaspoon of soda and two teaspoons of cream tartar sifted through it. Stir in one pint of berries and steam one hour. Serve with sauce.

CREAM PUDDING.

Mix with one and one-half cups of milk, two cups of flour and one teaspoon of salt. Beat three eggs to a froth, and just before baking add one cup of cream.

BAKED INDIAN PUDDING No. 1.

Two-thirds cup of Indian meal, one-third cup of flour, mixed together; two-thirds cup of molasses, one egg. Beat the egg in a bowl with the molasses and one teaspoonful of cassia, one large teaspoonful of suet, if you have, if not a small piece of butter; salt. Let one quart of milk come to a boil, leaving one pint to stir in with the egg, molasses and other ingredients. When the milk comes to a boil, stir in the meal and flour gradually. Let it stand and cool before you put in the egg, molasses, etc. Bake four hours.

INDIAN PUDDING No. 2.

One quart of scalding milk, one scant cup of meal. Stir the meal soft with the molasses, then stir into scalding milk a little salt and cinnamon and meal. Let cook a few minutes. Take off stove and add half pint cold milk. Bake slowly two hours.

BAKED INDIAN PUDDING No. 3.

Scald two quarts of milk, reserving one cupful cold, eight tablespoonfuls Indian meal, and one and one-half cups of molasses, one teaspoonful each of ginger, cinnamon and salt. Take from the stove and when sufficiently cool add the cup of milk, two eggs, butter size of an egg, one cup of stoned raisins. Bake three or four hours with cover. To be eaten hot with butter or cold with cream, which is much nicer.

We sell all popular Fruit Jars.

ROLY-POLY PUDDING FOR BERRIES OR FRUIT.

One pint of milk, one-half teaspoonful soda, one quart of flour, one teaspoonful cream tartar, butter size of an egg; cut it into flour; add milk and soda. Roll it one inch thick as soft as you can have it; spread berries or fruit over this; sprinkle with sugar; roll it up and steam one hour. Serve with sauce.

GINGERBREAD PUDDING.

One cup of molasses, one cup of sour milk, three cups of pastry flour, one tablespoon of butter, one tablespoon cinnamon, one teaspoon of soda, one-half teaspoon salt, one tablespoonful of vinegar. Mix molasses, butter and seasoning, dissolve soda in milk, add to the molasses, then add flour, lastly vinegar. Bake in tin pie plates if an inch thick, bake two minutes in a moderate oven.

Sauce: One egg, one-half cup powdered sugar, one-half teaspoon of vanilla, three tablespoons of milk. Beat white of egg stiff, beat in the sugar, then add vanilla, and the unbeaten yolk of the egg, lastly all the milk.

CIRCASSIAN PUDDING.

Boil six tablespoons of bread crumbs in one pint of milk. Stir in the yolks of three eggs beaten with four tablespoonfuls of sugar and piece of butter size of walnut. Take from the fire and stir in gradually the well beaten whites of three eggs. Flavor with vanilla, pour into buttered dish and bake in slow oven. Serve with sauce flavored with lemon juice.

ENGLISH PLUM PUDDING.

One large quart of milk, one dozen large crackers or fourteen small ones soaked in the milk over night. In the morning add one small cup of suet chopped fine, two cups of raisins, one cup of currants, six eggs, one teaspoon each of cloves, cinnamon and mace, one nutmeg, one and one-half cups of sugar, one cup of molasses. Steam five hours. This pudding will keep for weeks.

Mansfield's Pure Maple Syrup in Cans and Bottles.

RICE PUDDING.

One quart of milk, one cup of rice, one small cup molasses, one quarter of a teaspoon of salt. Bake slowly two hours or until the rice looks red like Indian meal.

CRUMB PUDDING

Six tablespoonfuls of soft bread crumbs, one pint of sweet milk, boil milk and bread ; stir until smooth, then cool. Add yolks of three eggs and three-quarters of a cup of sugar beaten together ; beat the whites of eggs and add last. Bake about forty minutes in a moderate oven.

Sauce: One cup of sugar, butter the size of a small walnut, cream together, and mix white of egg enough to make hard sauce. Flavor with vanilla or lemon juice.

FRUIT PUDDING.

One cup of molasses, one of sweet milk, one-half cup of melted butter, one of raisins, half a cup of currants, two and a half cups of flour, half a teaspoon of soda. Mix well. Salt and spice to taste and steam two hours.

CRACKER PUDDING.

Six crackers, three spoonfuls of melted butter, four spoonfuls of sugar and molasses, nutmeg and salt, one quart of milk scalded and poured over this. When cool, add four eggs, and chopped raisins. Serve with sauce.

ENGLISH PUDDING.

One cup of molasses, one-half cup of butter, one cup of sweet milk, one teaspoon of soda, three and one-half cups of flour, a teaspoon of different spices, one cup of chopped raisins, one-half cup of currants and citron. Steam two or three hours. Serve with sweet sauce.

BURNT CUSTARD PUDDING.

One quart of milk, four eggs, one-half cup of sugar. Cover the bottom of a two quart tin pan nearly an inch deep with damp brown sugar. Melt the sugar on the top of the stove, warm the custard and pour over it without stirring. Bake slowly. When cold turn out bottom up. Add a little salt. This is very nice.

Always use our Pastry Flour.

TURK'S CAPS.

Two eggs, one pint of milk, one pint of flour; salt, flavor to taste. Bake in cups half full. To be served hot with sugar and cream.

DELICIOUS PUDDING.

Thicken one pint of milk with one-half cup of flour, and simmer ten minutes. Add nearly a cup of sugar and a good half cup of butter; stir while hot until thoroughly mixed. When half cold add the beaten yolks of five eggs; when entirely cold, add whites of eggs beaten to a stiff froth. Flavor with lemon or vanilla. Bake in a two-quart dish as it rises a great deal. Place in a pan of hot water in a quick oven for half an hour. Serve with hard sauce flavored differently from pudding.

COTTAGE PUDDING.

One teacup of sweet milk, one cup of sugar, one egg, one tablespoonful of melted butter, one-half teaspoon of soda, three cups of flour. Bake one-half hour.

LEMON PUDDING.

Soak two slices of stale bread in cup of cold water. Mix the yolks of two eggs, one-half cup of melted butter, a scant cup of sugar and the juice of one lemon, and pour over the bread. Bake, and frost with the whites of two eggs and one cup of sugar. Brown lightly.

FRUIT PUDDING.

Two cups of chopped bread, one-half cup of chopped suet, one-half cup of molasses, one egg, one cup of stoned raisins, one cup of milk with one-half teaspoon of soda dissolved in it, one teaspoon of cloves, one of cinnamon, a little nutmeg and salt. Boil two hours in a double boiler.

Sauce: One-half cup of butter and one cup of sugar beaten to a cream; add one egg well beaten and five tablespoonfuls of boiling water. Put in a bowl and set in the top of the teakettle until it thickens.

BROWN BETTY.

One cup of bread crumbs, two cups of chopped apple, one-half cup of sugar; cinnamon, butter and salt. Butter a

We Warrant All Our Goods

pudding dish, and spread in layers, leaving the top layer of apple. Cover closely with a plate and bake one hour. Do not remove the plate until it has been out of the oven twenty minutes. Serve with any sauce.

PLUM PUDDING.

Two cups of raisins stoned and chopped, one-half cup of butter, one-half cup of sugar, one-half cup of molasses, one teaspoonful of soda, one teaspoonful of all kinds of spices, three eggs. White of one for cold sauce. Mix in flour enough to make it stiffer than molasses gingerbread; scant cup of buttermilk, with teaspoonful of soda. Steam four hours.

STEAMED BATTER PUDDING.

One cup of sweet milk, four cups of flour, two eggs, one cup of sugar, one teaspoonful of salt, two teaspoonfuls of cream tartar, one teaspoonful soda. Steam in cups thirty minutes. Can put any kind of fruit in them. Serve with sauce.

PUDDING SAUCE.

FOAM SAUCE No. 1.

Beat until light one cup of sugar and half cup of butter; add the grated rind of half a lemon, and pour over the mixture one cup of boiling milk. Let it stand twenty minutes.

FOAM SAUCE No. 2.

Scald a half cup of milk. While scalding beat a half cup of sugar and one egg very lightly, then pour in milk, flavor and et over steam of teakettle fifteen or twenty minutes.

SAUCE FOR PLUM PUDDING.

Two cups of sugar, two-thirds of a cup of butter, two teaspoons of flour, white of one egg, one-half pint of boiling water. Place in a pan of boiling water and stir until it thickens. Flavor to taste.

MOLASSES SAUCE.

One cup of molasses, two large spoons of sugar, one-half cup of vinegar; let it boil up once or twice, and then thicken with a dessert spoonful of flour which has been mixed with a

We always sell Revere Granulated Sugar

little of the molasses reserved. Boil about ten minutes; take from the fire and add a piece of butter the size of an egg.

FOAMING SAUCE.

Beat whites of three eggs to a stiff froth, melt a teacup of sugar in a little water and let it come to a boil; stir in one glass of wine and then the yolks of the eggs. Serve at once.

FRENCH SAUCE.

Cream half a pound of butter, and stir in half a pound of sugar. Then add the yolk of an egg and a gill of wine. Put it on the fire; stir till it simmers. Flavor with nutmeg.

A DELICIOUS BROWN SAUCE.

One-half pint of milk, one tablespoonful of butter, two tablespoonfuls of sugar, two tablespoonfuls of flour, and two tablespoonfuls of molasses. Boil ten minutes.

WINE SAUCE.

One and a half cups powdered sugar, two-thirds of a cup butter; beat to a stiff cream; add one wineglass of wine or vanilla or nutmeg or brandy and beaten white of an egg.

Families have perfect freedom to choose what sort of Preserves they will eat; they can buy tons of jelly and preserves for 10 cts., per pound, if they like that sort, or they can buy

ALONZO A. KNIGHTS' PRESERVES

Guaranteed to be made from Selected Fruits, Granulated Sugar, with no sort of adulteration.

Our advice is whether you have 10 cents or $10 to spend, buy the BEST as far as your money goes, and then eat plain bread and butter.

Cheap Luxuries are Not Desirable·

Always a large variety at

W. H. Mansfield & Co., Putnam.

LADIES!

Will you kindly try the

BOSTON CRYSTAL GELATINE?

It is double the strength of any other, is tasteless, odorless, and makes the most transparent jelly, and it costs you less than any other. Read what Prof. Sharples, State Assayer of Massachusetts, says of it.

[Letter]

S. P. Sharples, State Assayer, 13 Broad St.

Boston, Jan. 9, 1890.

Messrs. John A. Andrews & Co.:

Gentlemen—I have made a careful examination of the four samples of gelatine submitted to me in unbroken packages. These were marked:

    Boston Crystal Gelatine.
    Nelson's Improved Brilliant Gelatine.
    James Chalmers' Sons' Transparent Gelatine.
    Cox's Patent Refined Sparkling Gelatine.

As a result of this analysis, I find that the Boston Crystal Gelatine is superior to all the others, in that it is absolutely free from taste and odor, and that it makes a more transparent jelly. It yields nearly double the amount of jelly that the same weight of Cox's will produce, and considerably more than an equal weight of either of the others.

Respectfully,

(Signed,   S. P. SHARPLES.

For sale by W. H. Mansfield & Co.

COLD PUDDINGS.

CHOCOLATE BLANC MANGE.

One quart of milk, one-half box of gelatine, one square of chocolate. Dissolve the gelatine in cold water enough to cover it; set the dish of milk in hot water and let it boil, dissolving the chocolate in it, add gelatine and let it boil a few minutes before pouring into the mould. Better if made the day before using.

COLD BREAD PUDDING.

Cut in thin slices a small loaf of stale bread; wash and pick one pint of currants; butter the slices of bread. Put a layer of bread in the bottom of a pudding mould; sprinkle with the currants; put in more bread and crumbs until all is used. Beat four eggs and a half cup of sugar together, with one pint of milk and a little grated nutmeg; pour over the bread; let stand half an hour until brown; set away to cool and serve with cream sauce.

RASPBERRY CREAM ICE.

One quart of cream, one pint of milk, one pound of sugar, one lemon, one pound of raspberries. Mash the raspberries, and mix all the ingredients together, and strain into a freezer. Serve with wafers or sponge cake when frozen.

Bananas sliced with one cup of powdered sugar over them and the juice of one lemon, make a good dessert. Stand on ice one hour before used.

VANILLA CREAM.

One pint of sugar, one of water, three pints of cream not too rich, the yolks of five eggs and one large tablespoonful of vanilla extract. Boil the sugar and water together for twenty-five minutes. Beat the yolks of the eggs with one-fourth of a teaspoonful of salt. Place the basin of boiling syrup in another of boiling water. Stir the yolks of the eggs into the syrup, and beat rapidly for three minutes. Take the basin from the fire, place it in a pan of ice water, and beat until cold. Add the vanilla and cream, and freeze.

Use Boston Crystal Gelatine.

CARAMEL ICE CREAM.

Make the hot mixture as for vanilla. Put the small cupful of sugar in a small frying pan, and stir over the fire until the sugar turns liquid and begins to smoke. Turn into the boiling mixture and put way to cool. When cold add one quart of cream. Strain the mixture into the freezer and freeze. The flavor of this cream can be varied by browning the sugar more or less.

SPANISH CREAM.

One pint of milk, put on in double boiler and dissolve in it half a box of gelatine; when the gelatine is fully dissolved add the yolks of three eggs, beaten, and five tablespoons of sugar. When it is as thick as custard, take from the stove and add the whites of the eggs beaten stiff, and vanilla. Put in mould to cool.

PHILADELPHIA ICE CREAM.

Take three pints of milk, when it comes to a boil stir in two tablespoons of flour mixed in cold milk. Cook twenty minutes. When cold add one quart of cream, two and one-half cups of sugar, vanilla and a little salt.

PEACH PUDDING.

One-half box of gelatine soaked in enough cold water to cover it. Make a custard of one pint of milk, two eggs, one-half cup of sugar; let it cool and add gelatine. When almost cold add one pint of peaches, either fresh or canned, pour into a mould. Serve with whipped cream flavored with the peach juice. Raspberries may be used in place of peaches.

CORN STARCH PUDDING.

One large pint of boiling water, whites of three eggs beaten to a froth, a little salt, three tablespoons of corn starch mixed in a little water; mix starch in first, then eggs, cook a few minutes, beating steadily.

Sauce: Yolks of three eggs, three-quarters of a cup of sugar, one cup of milk, one tablespoon of butter, vanilla, a little flour for thickening. Boil milk, beat the rest and add.

Be Careful about Flavoring Extracts.

APPLE SNOW PUDDING.

One large baked apple (tart), white of one egg, one cup of sugar. Beat all together three-quarters of an hour.

Sauce: One cup of milk (boiling), add to it the yolk of one egg, two or three tablespoons of sugar, one teaspoon of flour. Cook until thick. After cooling, flavor to taste.

FRUIT JELLY.

To one ounce package of Boston Crystal Gelatine add one pint of cold water, place over the tea kettle or any warm place. To one tea cup of dried apricots, or other fruit, put one quart of cold water and place on back of the stove to slowly swell. When the fruit is quite soft, let it boil slowly a few minutes (never stir it and the jelly will be clear), add two cups of sugar; boil two minutes, and carefully skim the fruit into a mould. Put the gelatine into the syrup, and just let it boil up, and pour over the fruit. When cold serve with cream and sugar.

JUDGE PETERS' PUDDING.

Three-quarters of a box of gelatine, two lemons, two oranges, six figs, nine dates, two bananas, ten nuts of any kind; dissolve the gelatine in one-half pint of cold water for one hour; add then one-half pint of boiling water, the juice of two lemons, and two cups of sugar. Strain and let it stand until it begins to thicken. Stir into this all the fruit cut into small pieces, and let it harden. Pour into a mould.

JELLIED PRUNES.

Use one pint of prunes, a pint and a half of water, one-half a package of gelatine, one-half pint of wine and one of sugar. Soak the gelatine in one gill of the water for two hours; wash the prunes in two waters, rubbing them well between the hands; put in a stewpan with five gills of water and cook slowly for one hour; take up the prunes and remove the stones; return the fruit to the water in the stewpan and let it boil up; add the gelatine and take from the fire, stir until gelatine is dissolved, then add sugar and wine. Place the stewpan in a pan of ice water and stir the preparation until it begins to thicken. Pour into a mould and set in

Headquarters for Prunes, Figs, &c.

a cool place to harden. It should stand four or five hours. Served with soft custard or whipped cream.

PEACH CREAM.

One pint of cream, whipped, add sugar to taste, one half can of peaches cut up and stirred into the cream. Add one-third of a box of gelatine dissolved in a little warm water. Place in mould to harden.

FROZEN PEACHES.

One dozen large ripe peaches, one cup of water, one of sugar, the whites of six eggs beaten stiff; cut the peaches into small bits and stir down from the sides frequently while freezing.

TAPIOCA CREAM.

Cover three tablespoonfuls of tapioca (over night) with cold water. In the morning pour off the water, and put into one quart of milk in a double boiler over the fire. Stir into it the yolks of four eggs with two-thirds of a cup or sugar and a little salt. Stir until it begins to thicken. When cool flavor with vanilla. Make a frosting of the whites of the eggs and drop over the top; sprinkle over a little sugar. Put in the oven and brown lightly.

ORANGE PUDDING.

One and one-half cups of sugar, yolks of six eggs, one quart of milk, one-half box of gelatine soaked in one-half pint of milk one hour; eight oranges. Boil one and one-half pints of milk. Beat yolks and sugar together, add a little cold milk to prevent it curdling, a little salt, pour on boiling milk. In another kettle add gelatine and set on fire, stirring until it boils, and set away to cool. Pare and divide oranges and pour custard over them. Beat whites stiff and add six tablespoons of sugar and flavor with one teaspoon of orange juice. Pour this over the top and serve.

GELATINE PUDDING.

One pint of milk. Separate whites and yolks of four eggs; with the yolks make a boiled custard. Soak one-third of a box of gelatine a few minutes in cold water, then add

We always carry a choice selection of Fruits

three-quarters of a cup of boiling water; when the custard has cooled, add the gelatine water, whites of four eggs. Stir well together. Flavor with vanilla. Cool in a mould.

PINEAPPLE SPONGE.

One fresh pineapple or a pint and a half of the fruit, one cupful of sugar, one-half package of gelatine, one and one-half cupfuls of water, the whites of four eggs. Soak the gelatine two hours in a cupful of the water; chop the pineapple fine, put it and the juice in a tin with the sugar and remainder of water. Simmer ten minutes, add the gelatine, take from the fire and when partially cooled, add the whites of the eggs beaten stiff; beat until the mixture begins to thicken; pour into a mould and set away to harden. Serve with whipped cream.

ORANGE SHERBET.

Mix together one pint of orange juice, the grated yellow rind of two oranges and the juice of two lemons. Let this mixture stand one hour, strain and freeze. or the sugar and water may be boiled together for twenty minutes, the strained fruit juice added to this, cool and freeze.

Lemon Sherbet is made the same way, using lemons in place of oranges

FANCY WAY OF SERVING THE SHERBET.

Cut a slice from the top of the orange of lemon, remove the inside with a spoon, and use for the sherbet. Into this shell put the frozen sherbet, and serve on a plate with a doily under it.

JELLIED APPLES.

Use two quarts of tart apples, peeled. quartered and cored; two cupfuls of sugar, one lemon, half a package of gelatine, and one pint and a half of water. Soak the gelatine in half a cupful of water for two hours. Put the sugar, lemon juice and the remainder of the water on the stove, and boil rapidly for ten minutes, then put in as many apples as may be cooked without crowding, cook gently until so tender they can be pierced with a broom straw, then take up

Don't forget Victor Flour

with a skimmer and spread on a platter; put more apples into a stewpan, and contnuie cooking until all are done. When the last of the fruit has been taken up, remove the pan from the fire and put the gelatine into it; stir until the gelatine is dissolved, then place the stewpan in a basin containing ice water, stir until cool. Put in the apples, mix, turn into a mould and set in a cool place to harden. Serve with whipped cream or soft custard.

LEMON CREAM PUDDING.

Beat the yolks of four eggs with four tablespoonfuls of sugar; add the juice and grate rind of one large lemon, and two tablespoonfuls of hot water. Place a tin containing the above within a spider of boiling water, simmer till it thickens, then remove from the fire and stir in the whites of the four eggs beaten stiff with two tablespoonfufs of sugar. Eat cold.

AMHERST PUDDING.

One cup of molasses, one cup of milk, one cup chopped raisins, one cup of suet or three-quarters of a cup of butter, one teaspoonful of all kinds of spices, one teaspoonful soda; flour sufficient for a tolerablely stiff batter, about three and one-half cups.

KINGSLEY PUDDING

Three pints of milk, yolks of four eggs, one-half box of gelatine, sweeten and flavor to taste, boil like a custard. As it is taken from the fire, stir in the whites of four eggs beaten to a froth and stir while cooling. Before it thickens put in a dozen each of macaroons and cocoanut drops and let it harden. Eat cold. This makes a large pudding

SNOW PUDDING.

To one small box of Boston Crystal Gelatine, add one-half cup cold water, soak half an hour, then add one cup of boiling water to dissolve gelatine, juice of three lemons, and one cup of sugar. Beat the whites of four eggs stiff, and when the gelatine is cold not stiff, pour it into the egg, and beat it till it will just drop from a spoon, then pour in a

Largest Variety of Freserves

mould. Set away to cool. The custard poured over it in serving is made as follows : One pint of milk, yolks of four eggs, two tablespoons of sugar, grated rind of one lemon. Boil five minutes.

WINE JELLY

To one package of gelatine add one pint of cold water; let it stand ten minutes to soak, with sticks of cinnamon in it. One pint of sugar and nearly one cup of wine, then pour in two pints and one-half of boiling water; put over the fire and let it come to a boil; take off and strain, adding a cup more of wine and juice of a lemon or two.

LEMON JELLY.

Pour one quart of boiling water over three-quarters of a box of gelatine: let it dissolve, then add one and one-half pounds of sugar, and the juice of three lemons. Strain into mould.

ORANGE JELLY.

Dissolve one-half box of gelatine in one cup of cold water for ten minutes, add two cups of boiling water, one cup of sugar, juice of six oranges and two lemons. Strain into moulds.

CHARLOTTE RUSSE NO. 1.

Line a glass dish with slices of any plain cake (sponge cake is best). Make a custard as follows: A pint of rich milk, yolk of two eggs and one whole one, a half cup of sugar, a pinch of salt. Boil, and flavor with vanilla; when cool, pour over the sliced cake. Just before serving beat the whites previously reserved; when stiff add two tablespoonfuls of sugar, and a few drops of vanilla; spread over the custard. Lastly cut small squares of jelly and drop them on the white frosting.

CHARLOTTE RUSSE NO. 2.

One-half box of gelatine, one coffee cup of milk, whites of two eggs, small half cup of sugar, half pint of thick cream. Soak the gelatine in a litte cold water, scald the milk and pour over it, strain, then add the sugar and eggs beaten to a

Crystal Gelatine, cheapest and best

stiff froth. When cool add the cream beaten to a stiff froth. Flavor with vanilla. Line the mould with sponge cake, fill and put in a cool place.

CREAM CUSTARD.

Scald one quart of milk and pour into it the following mixture, stirring constantly, till thickened: Yolks of four eggs, beaten with two-thirds of a cup of sugar and three teaspoonfuls of flour. Flavor with vanilla. Beat the whites with one tablespoon of sugar to a stiff froth, then pour the custard into a pudding dish. Dip the frosting out with a tablespoon and put on the top; set in the oven and brown, then put one teaspoonful of jelly in the top of each spoonful of frosting.

RICE PUDDING.

Boil one-half cup of rice in one quart of milk until soft— about one hour—and then add the yolks of three eggs beaten light with one-half cup of sugar, a little salt, and a teaspoonful of vanilla. Frost with whites.

ORANGE FLOAT.

Mix one quart of water, the juice and pulp of two lemons, and one coffee cup of sugar. Boil sufficiently to dissolve the sugar and then strain and again bring to a boil. Add four tablespoonfuls of cornstarch, mixed in a little cold water, stir and boil fifteen minutes; when cool, pour it over four or five slices of oranges; on the top spread the beaten whites of three eggs sweetened, and flavored with vanilla. Eat with cream.

CHOCOLATE CREAM

One quart of milk, three-quarters of a cup of sugar, yolks of three eggs, one-quarter of a cake of chocolate, one-half package of gelatine. Put the gelatine into cold milk and let it stand one hour. Cook same as custard. Put the eggs and sugar in last well beaten together. Cook ten minutes. Frost with whites.

Very finest Butter always in Stock

We lead the trade on

FINE ✠ TEAS

From Medium to High Grades.

We always buy from the Importers and get Best Choice, and sell same on their merits.

NO PRESENTS !

Remember, when you get a present with your tea, you have to pay for it every time, and pretty dearly, too. These prize tea peddlers are not public benefactors; they must get their profit, and the firm supplying also. How? By making you pay them from 25 to 50 per cent. more than our prices would be for same grade of goods, if we should lower ourselves enough to handle such trash.

Don't take our word for above, but compare ours with the prize tea, and you cannot fail to see the great difference.

W. H. MANSFIELD & CO.

HEADQUARTERS FOR

DRIED FRUITS

Consisting of

Table and Cooking

Raisins,

Currants,

Citron,

Prunes, Figs, Dates,

Of California, Sultana, Malaga, Valencia, and Turkey Varieties.

Very Finest Brands obtainable at

W. H. MANSFIELD & CO'S

CANDY.

VANILLA CARAMELS.

Two cups of sugar, one cup of milk, one quarter teaspoonful of cream tartar. Boil until hard. Flavor with vanilla, but do not stir; pour into pan and when cool cut into small squares.

MOLASSES CANDY.

Two cups of molasses, one tablespoonful of sugar. Stir occasionally while boiling; before taking from the stove add butter half the size of an egg, and one-third teaspoonful of soda. Pour into buttered tins and when cool enough pull it.

WHITE CARAMELS.

Two cups sugar, one cup of milk, butter size of an egg, one teaspoon of vanilla. Boil slowly fifteen minutes. Beat until cool enough to pour over the chocolate.

WALNUT CARAMELS.

Two cups of sugar, one cup of milk, butter size of an egg, one pound of English walnuts cut in slices. Boil about ten minutes.

LAKE KISSES.

Two cups of white sugar, one cup of water, two tablespoonfuls of vinegar, butter size of an egg, a pinch of cream tartar, one teaspoonful of vanilla. Do not stir at all, and boil until it will harden in cold water. When cool enough, stretch and cut with scissors in small pieces.

BUTTER SCOTCH No. 1.

Two cups of sugar, four tablespoons molasses, four tablespoons water, one-half cup of vinegar. Cook until it hardens, then add one-half cup of butter. Flavor with vanilla. Pour into buttered tins and cut in squares.

All Kinds of Nuts, Figs and Dates.

BUTTER SCOTCH No. 2.

Two cups of sugar, a cup of butter half cup of vinegar, 1-4 cup of molasses. Boil till very thick and brittle, then one teaspoon of vanilla and pour very thin on buttered tins. Very nice peanut taffy can be made from this by omitting the vanilla and adding two quarts peanuts.

CHOCOLATE CARAMELS No. 1.

Two cups of sugar, one half cup of molasse. one-half cup of milk, butter half the size of an egg, not quite two squares of chocolate. Boil about ten minutes, then take from the stove and beat until it sugars around the edge of the dish. Pour in pans and cool.

CHOCOLATE CARAMELS No. 2.

Two cups of sugar. one scant cup of molasses. one-half cup of milk. Boil fifteen minutes; when nearly done stir in four squares of chocolate and a piece of butter. Flavor with vanilla.

CHOCOLATE CARAMELS No. 3.

Two cups of sugar, two-thirds of a cup of milk, two-thirds of a cup of molasses, butter size of an egg, two squares of chocolate, two teaspoons of vanilla. Cook slowly twenty minutes, then beat till cool.

PEPPERMINTS.

Two and one-half cups of sugar and one-half cup of milk. Boil four minutes, take from the fire and add one teaspoon of peppermint. Beat steadily till it will harden upon paraffine paper without running. Drop on, a teaspoonful at a time, as quickly as possible. If the last sugars in the saucepan before it can be used, add milk and put upon the stove again for a few minutes.

CREAM CANDY.

One pound of white sugar. one wineglassful of vinegar, one tumbler of water, vanilla; boil half an hour. Pull if you like.

Use Rockwood's Chocolate.

DRINKS.

PICNIC COFFEE.

One pound coffee, one-fourth Mocha and three-fourths Java, two eggs, shell and all, mixed with the dry coffee. Stir well with a spoon, then add two gallons of cold water. Let it cook slowly only boiling up once or twice, then put it on the back of the stove. Put in a cup of cold water and pour out a little to see that the nozzle is not filled with grounds.

CHOCOLATE.

Tablespoonful of chocolate for each person. Pour on boiling water and allow it to thicken; milk enough to cool; then stir in a well beaten egg; sugar to taste. Add milk and boil fifteen minutes; flavor with vanilla. Beat whites of eggs and pour over when ready to serve.

TEA.

One teaspoonful of tea for each person; add boiling water, do not boil, only steep it. It can be made on the table the same way.

COCOA.

Put one-half teaspoon of Bensdorp's soluble cocoa in a breakfast cup with a teaspoon of sugar, mix, and pour on a little boiling water. Then fill cup with scalded milk and boiling water.

COCOA No. 2,

One teaspoonful of Rockwood's (or any breakfast cocoa), mixed well with tablespoonful of boiling water; add equal quantities scalded milk and water. Boil three minutes, and sweeten to taste. One teaspoon cocoa to a cup.

LEMONADE.

One pound of sugar to one dozen lemons, three oranges, large piece of ice, one glass of water to a lemon. One bottle of Apollinaris water or a siphon of Vichy in place of water improves it.

Apollinaris and Ross' Ginger Ale.

PICKLES.

SWEET TOMATO PICKLE

One peck of green tomatoes, six onions sliced, sprinkle over this one cup of salt over night. In morning drain off water, then add two quarts of water, one quart of vinegar; boil fifteen minutes, then drain off this water and throw away. Take two quarts of vinegar, two pounds of sugar, two tablespoons cloves, two of ginger, two of mustard, two of cinnamon, one-quarter teaspoon cayenne pepper; put spice in a bag. Cook fifteen minutes.

TOMATO KETCHUP No. 1.

Twelve large tomatoes, ripe, six onions, three peppers, two tablespoons brown sugar, one pint of vinegar, salt to taste. Chop onions and peppers and cook slowly two hours. Bottle while hot.

TOMATO KETCHUP No. 2.

Eight quarts strained tomatoes, six tablespoonfuls of salt, four tablespoonfuls of black pepper, three tablespoonfuls of mustard, one tablespoonful of ground cloves, one tablespoonful of ginger, one quart of vinegar, one-half cup of brown sugar, one tumbler of brandy. Boil very gently until the quantity is reduced one-half. Put into bottles.

PICKLED PEARS.

Eight pounds of pears, four pounds of brown sugar, one ounce of cinnamon and cloves, one quart of vinegar. Steam the pears until soft, stick a few cloves in each; boil the sugar, vinegar and spice and pour over the fruit hot. Repeat this process three times. Let them stand five days each time.

Buy Your Vinegar and Spices of Us

CUCUMBER PICKLES.

The small, long kind are best for pickles, and those but half-grown are nicer than the full grown. Let them be freshly gathered, pull off the blossom, but do not rub them. Pour over them a strong brine boiling hot, cover closely, and let them stand all night. In the morning drain on a sieve, and dry them in a cloth. To each quart of cider vinegar put one-half ounce of whole black pepper, the same of ginger and allspice, and one ounce of mustard seed,—add onions if agreeable. When this pickled vinegar boils up, throw in the cucumbers, and make them boil as quickly as possible for three or four minutes—no longer. Put them in a jar with the boiling vinegar and cover closely. Made in this way your pickles will be tender, crisp and green. If the color is not quite clear enough, boil the vinegar over the next day, then put on the cucumbers and cover perfectly tight.

CHUTNEY SAUCE.

Four pounds of sliced apples, one quart of vinegar, one pound of brown sugar, one cup of stoned raisins, one cup of currants, one cup of sliced citron, four ounces of peppers, four ounces of garlic, pounded, two ounces of salt. cook until soft. When cold, bottle.

SPICED GRAPES.

Squeeze the pulp of the grapes out of the skins. Cook the pulp a few minutes until you can press it all through a sieve. Reject the seeds. Add a little water to the skins and cook till they are quite tender. Then make a syrup of three pounds of sugar, one pint of vinegar, two tablespoons of cinnamon, two tablespoons of clove and half a teaspoon of salt. Add the grapes (this quantity is for six pounds), and boil fifteen minutes.

CHILI SAUCE No. 1.

Nine large, ripe tomatoes; scald, peel and chop with one pepper and one large onion. Add one tablespoonful of salt,

Tomatoes, Peppers, Onions in the Season

two of sugar and one each of ginger, cloves, allspice and cinnamon, one nutmeg, two small cups of vinegar. Stew one hour and bottle while hot.

CHILI SAUCE No. 2.

Twelve ripe tomatoes, two onions, four peppers (or one tablespoon of cayenne), four cups of vinegar, one-half cup of sugar. Chop onions, tomatoes and peppers fine (first skin the tomatoes. Boil one hour.

SPICED CURRANTS.

Five pounds of ripe currants, four pounds of sugar, two tablespoons each of cloves, cinnamon and allspice, one pint of vinegar. Boil three hours until quite thick.

PICKLED FIGS.

Two pounds of sugar to one pint of vinegar, one ounce of cinnamon, one half ounce of cloves. Cook thoroughly and pour over the figs while hot. Let stand twenty-four hours, pour off and cook over into a syrup; Repeat this six or eight times.

CUCUMBER KETCHUP.

Grate one dozen large cucumbers, without paring, squeeze and to this pulp add two small onions, chopped; two quarts of vinegar, salt and pepper to taste.

Every Department

In our Store contains a finer assortment than any house outside of the cities. We aim to carry the best grades, and as many brands of same, as our trade will allow.

We do not advertise to sell our goods lower than any house in the State, but we do say that no house carries any better goods in Eastern Connecticut.

Then again we guarantee all goods, and thus a customer runs no risk on poor goods.

If you are not our customer, become so at once, and it will be appreciated by

W. H. MANSFIELD & CO.

USEFUL HINTS.

To prevent sleeplessness after drinking coffee at night: Eat a pickle or lemon to counteract the effect.

To remove ink from woolen fabrics, put on sugar immediately and let it absorb all it will, then brush off and put on more sugar until all the ink is absorbed.

To take out iron stains, put on lemon juice and salt and lay in the sun.

There is scarcely any ache to which children are subject so bad to bear as the earache. But there is a remedy never known to fail. Take a bit of cotton batting, put upon it a pinch of black pepper, gather it up and tie it, dip in sweet oil and insert into the ear. Put a flannel bandage over the head to keep it warm. It will give immediate relief.

If onions are sliced and kept in a sick room they will absorb all the atmospheric poison. They should be changed every hour. In the room of a small-pox patient they blister and decompose very rapidly, but will prevent the spread of the disease. Their application has also proved effectual in the case of snake bites.

A POWERFUL POULTICE.—Wounds made by rusty tools or nails, or by the teeth of dogs and other animals, are not only very painful but generally quite dangerous. To allay the pain, extract the poison and hasten the healing process, there is nothing that we know of so wonderfully effective as raw, fat salt salt pork and onions, equal parts, chopped up together and applied in a thick layer either directly to the wound or first folded into a single layer of linen. Leave on until healed. Even a slice of raw salt pork, tied over the wound made by a rusty nail, will draw the inflammation all out, render the flesh clear white, and heal up the injury quicker than any drug, known to us, will do it. This is the best use that can be made of fat pork, as we do not believe in its free internal application, especially in summer.

STAINS UPON LINEN AND COTTON.—In nearly all cases, stains may be removed by means of chloride of lime, which sub-

Remember Victor Flour.

stance is sufficiently common to be had of every druggist. It is applied thus: Dissolve about two teaspoonfuls of the chloride of lime in a quart of water; take another portion of water and make it perceptibly sour by the addition of white vinegar—the ordinary brown vinegar will do nearly as well; now well wet the stained or discolored articles with the sour water, then put them into the solution of the chloride of lime; perfect bleaching will then take place in from ten to twenty minutes; in some instances the operation must be repeated once or twice; finally, well rinse in plenty of clean water. The omission of the vinegar is the chief reason why so many persons fail in their attempts to bleach with chloride of lime.

Cream of tartar rubbed upon soiled white kid gloves cleanses them well.

Musty bottles or jars may be sweetened with lye or dissolved soda. Let either remain in them a short time, then dry and scald them. They will not become musty if a little salt be kept in them.

RELIEF FROM BURNS.—To obtain quick relief from burns, apply a layer of common salt and saturate it with laudanum. Hold it in position a few hours with a simple wrapper. The smarting disappears almost immediately, and the sore gets well with incredible rapidity.

GREASE FROM SILK AND VELVET.—Rub the spot on the silk or velvet lightly and rapidly with a clean, soft cotton rag dipped in ether. Repeat the operation if necessary. Finish with a clean, dry cloth. Rub lightly and rapidly, or else a slight stain will be the result. We have known grease spots to be taken out of the most delicate colored silks in the way described.

TO WASH BLANKETS.—Have an abundance of hot water in which borax has been dissolved, and a small quantity of Old Reliable soap—never use soap with rosin in it, as rosin always hardens the fibre of wool. Put the ends into the washer, and then put in the blankets after all the dirt has been

Use Old Reliable Tomatoes.

removed, wring into another tub of hot suds, and from that wring into a tub of hot bluing water; wring from this and hang at once in the open air to dry. If the water is abundant and soft, and you use this soap, blankets thus washed will not shrink, and will be as soft and fleecy as when they came from the store.

To Relieve a Cough.—For a dry, hacking cough, two or three times a day take a little pinch of salt, let it dissolve slowly on the tongue and swallow.

Another: Take five cents' worth of pulverized licorice extract and ground flaxseed; mix together, put a little in a cup: add strained honey to sweeten well, steep in hot water till licorice is dissolved. Take a good dose of it as often as the cough is troublesome. It is a sure, safe, speedy relief. Try it once.

For sick headache: Two teaspoonfuls of finely pulverized charcoal in half a glass of water.

To Restore Old Crape.—Skimmed milk and water, with a bit of glue in it, made scalding hot, is excellent to restore old rusty black Italian crape. If clapped and pulled dry, like muslin, it will look as well or better than new.

To Clean Flat Irons.—Beeswax and salt will make rusty flat irons as clean and smooth as glass. Tie a lump of wax in a rag and keep it for that purpose. When the irons are hot, rub them first with the wax rag, then scour them with a paper or cloth sprinkled with salt.

To Clean Black Cashmere.—Wash in hot suds, with a little borax in the water; rinse in bluing water—very blue—and iron while damp. It will look equal to new. Or, brush the article to be cleaned, and then wash in clear, cold water, and a handful of common washing soda, dissolved; use no soap or warm water. Iron on the wrong side while damp.

To Wash Calico.—Make flour starch as for ordinary starching, being sure that it is entirely free from lumps. This, of course, can be guarded against by straining the starch. Add enough to the clean water in which the gar-

Old Reliable Soap is Strictly Pure.

ments are to be washed to make it a little soft and a little slippery to the hand. Do not use soap, nor let the fabrics lie or soak in the water, but wash them out quickly. Add a little of the starch in the same way to the rinsing water, wring dry, and hang up without more starch. Black calico or cambric dresses washed thus will look nearly as fresh as new, and so of all colors; the only precaution needed is not to get too much of the starch in the wash water. Practice will soon teach this.

INDEX.

Bread,	47—52
Cake,	55—69
Cookies and Gingerbread,	73—76
Candy,	99—100
Cold Puddings,	88—96
Drinks,	101
Eggs.	38—40
Fish,	12—16
Hot Puddings.	82—87
Meats,	25—31
Pies and Pastry,	78—81
Pickles,	102—104
Poultry,	19—22
Salad,	40—43
Soups.	5—9
Sauces.	17—18
Vegetables,	33—37
Useful Hints,	105—107

www.ingramcontent.com/pod-product-compliance
Lightning Source LLC
Chambersburg PA
CBHW020146170426
43199CB00010B/909